# JUST BETWEEN US

# JUST BETWEEN US

## MARIO LOPEZ

with Steve Santagati

A CELEBRA BOOK

Celebra
Published by the Penguin Group
Penguin Group (USA) LLC, 375 Hudson Street,
New York, New York 10014

USA | Canada | UK | Ireland | Australia | New Zealand | India | South Africa | China
penguin.com
A Penguin Random House Company

First published by Celebra,
a division of Penguin Group (USA) LLC

First Printing, October 2014

LIBRARY OF CONGRESS CATALOGING-IN-PUBLICATION DATA:

Lopez, Mario, 1973–
Just between us/Mario Lopez.
   p. cm.
ISBN 978-0-451-47023-2
1. Lopez, Mario, 1973– 2. Television actors and actresses—United States. I. Title.
PN2287.L635A3 2014
791.4502'8092—dc23      2014016176
[B]

Printed in the United States of America
10   9   8   7   6   5   4   3   2   1

Set in Bulmer
Designed by Spring Hoteling

To my children, Gia Francesca and Dominic . . .
now you know where your old man came from.

When I was a child, I spoke, thought, and reasoned like a child. But when I became a man, I put away childish things.

—Corinthians 13:11

# CONTENTS

PROLOGUE.

You Are Here

1

CHAPTER 1.

Straight Outta Chula

9

CHAPTER 2.

Child Actor

45

CHAPTER 3.

*Saved by the Bell*

69

CHAPTER 4.

*Mi Vida Loca*

91

# CONTENTS

CHAPTER 5.

## Life After A. C. Slater

115

CHAPTER 6.

## Turning Points

143

CHAPTER 7.

## So You Think You Can Host?

181

CHAPTER 8.

## Mazza

213

ENCORE.

## Just Between Us

251

## Acknowledgments

259

# JUST BETWEEN US

PROLOGUE

# YOU ARE HERE

Every now and then, the universe has an uncanny way of reaching out, tapping me on the shoulder, and bringing me back down to earth. Sometimes the message is delivered to remind me of something that I've forgotten or maybe just to grab my attention in the midst of my usual action-packed schedule. Other times I feel the tap more as a big jolt that leads to an important discovery or decision—like the realization that hits me early one morning as I'm getting ready to hike one of my favorite trails at Griffith Park.

I love this park for the sheer amount of urban wilderness it contains, a refreshing break from the sprawl of Los Angeles. It's also practically in my backyard, so it's perfect for an early-morning hike and a good workout.

By the time I arrive at the park and start to stretch, it's just past six a.m. Not long after dawn, the sun has only just begun to come up. Bleary eyed, I definitely could have used that extra half hour of sleep. It's true: as committed as I am to a daily fitness regimen, I am no fan of the five thirty a.m. alarm. Then again, this happens to be the only time to get in a little workout before the demands of the day kick in. And there's something I love about the solitude of these early hours. The quiet is such that my inner thoughts seem like another person standing right beside me, talking and offering wise counsel.

Well, at least that's how it feels in these moments as I finish stretching and head over to a large park map in order to look for directions to the trail I plan to run. Standing there, I scan the map until my eyes land on the mark that shows where I am, pointing out the spot with bold red arrows and the words "You Are Here."

Those three words, intended to state the obvious, do have a kind of congratulatory vibe. Wouldn't it be helpful, I think, if we could start every day with a map and a marker to tell us: "You Are Here"?

That's when I feel the proverbial tap on my shoulder.

My first reaction is to ask myself if, as the map tells me, I am *here*, where exactly is that? More to the point: how did I get here? In truth, these aren't easy questions to answer. But seeing as I'm about to hit the milestone birthday of forty—a big one—I realize that's cause for reflection. Cliché as that may sound, it's one of those rites of passages that suddenly bring me face-to-face with the past and a life lived, for the most part, at full throttle.

It's hard to ignore the message of "You Are Here"—it's time to slow down, look back, and take stock of my life so far. All of it: the choices, the triumphs and defeats, the smart moves and the mistakes, and everything in between. Daunting as that can be, as I start up the trail that leads to a summit, I accept that only by recalling where I came from will I be able to see more clearly than ever where I am, who I am, and where I'm headed.

A couple of miles later, as I reach the top, the sun has broken through the marine layer and I can't help but smile as I look out at the sprawl of LA spread out below me. And that's when the idea for sharing my story, no holds barred, is first conceived.

When I glance over my shoulder at the long stretch of road I've taken—curving and winding from my childhood in the Latino community of Chula Vista, just outside of San Diego, all the way to the "You Are Here" map in the same park not far from the Hollywood sign—I smile, I laugh out loud, and sometimes I want to cry.

I've been in show business since I was ten years old. I've worked in almost every arena of the entertainment industry: as a kid in numerous commercials and TV series, as a teen actor who came of age in hundreds of episodes of *Saved by the Bell*, as both a guest star and leading young man in a bevy of projects made for television and film, as a triple-threat stage performer on Broadway, as both a contestant and a guest judge on *Dancing with the Stars*, and, of course, as the host of *Extra* and in an array of other hosting roles, in all of which I've spent hundreds upon hundreds of hours interviewing countless celebrities and Hollywood luminaries. In recent years, I've added other endeavors to the list—as the host of my own nationally syndicated radio show and as a producer with pots simmering on multiple burners. As an entrepreneur, I can assure you that many of the lessons learned along the way have been hard won. And as a loving husband and devoted father—my most important roles—I can also say that recognizing what truly matters in life is chief among those lessons.

There are a few reasons I chose to take on the challenge of putting down in words not just what happened in my story but how I felt at the time and especially what I learned in the process. At the top of the list was for me to make sense of *mi vida loca*—my crazy life—as it has been at times. Writing allows you the space to sit down, have a drink, and open yourself up to the memories. It's about retracing your steps to gain a deeper understanding of the journey, maybe for the first time ever.

Another reason I'm writing is to acknowledge the champions and mentors who have been there for me at every important turning point. Hopefully, I can pay it forward by sharing with you the same brand of encouragement and belief I was given. Whatever your aspirations, I hope that my experiences might prove valuable for your own journey.

As the pages ahead will show, I've made my share of mistakes. No one is perfect and I'm a prime example. But at my core, I've always lived by the values that my parents instilled in me and ultimately, mistakes and all, I'm proud of who I am and what I've done. Once I found my path and the goals that inspired me to pursue them with passion and purpose, I worked hard, giving my all. And now, man, I'm living my dream, proof of my hard work and damn good luck.

Without question, there have been highs and lows. But life is not really about arriving at that one spot marked "You Are Here." It's about all the choices you make in getting there and about the consequences of those choices. That's why I've decided to divulge certain stories that include intimate subject matter, some of which has to do with stupid and sometimes heartbreaking mistakes that still haunt me to this day. There are no do-overs in life, so I had to learn to pick myself up and move forward, never forgetting the lessons learned.

At first, I was not prepared for how difficult it is to bare your soul on paper. The feeling of being exposed and vulnerable caught me off guard. So did the need to write without counting characters like on Twitter or second-guessing that last click of the send button. I soon saw that this was going to take trust and confidence to put myself out there in such a candid way. Then, after I got past my own resistance, came pushback from my agents, managers, and publicists. The buzzing in my ear from well-intentioned counsel was clear: "No, Mario, you can't *say* that. Think of your image." "No, Mario, you can't *do* that; it could ruin your career."

Usually I listen, but this time I couldn't. These are my stories to tell. I didn't decide to change certain details to protect the innocent because, in Hollywood, no one is innocent. And, besides, as I've learned over the years, the truth is powerful. That's a lesson I rank high under the heading of "Things I Know Now That I Wish I Knew Then." As tempting as it is to tell people what they want to hear, I know now that the truth is the best response to every situation. Dishonesty takes too much out of life, and you don't have to use your memory as much.

By sharing a few of these lessons—call them truisms, or "Marioisms"—I hope to show that the experience that comes with age is a good teacher. And what I've had to learn many times is the truth that life is not fair. That doesn't mean that life is bad or not fun. It means that if you spend your time looking for "fair" you'll be missing out on a lot. All you can do is learn from the mistakes, bring your best to every endeavor, and strive to make choices that let you feel proud of yourself.

A big one on that list for me right now, if I had it to do all over again, is that I would have kept a better journal; some of the names and details that I would love to remember have vanished with age. I'm sure that in writing this book I have neglected to mention significant individuals and the stories that go along with them.

Along with sharing my own journey, I've also chosen to lift the velvet ropes to give you an insider's look at show business. In the world of money and privilege, Hollywood lives are supposed to be the height of glamour. But that's not the whole story. No one is famous forever, so you just have to make the most of every moment and every opportunity, no matter how much money you have today, no matter how many people recognize you as you walk down the street.

My life is in no way as glamorous as you might assume. At my house, where my amazing, gorgeous wife, Courtney, and I are raising our two beautiful children—our three-year-old daughter, Gia, and our infant son, Dominic—the time we spend together is the same as it is for most folks. On Sundays, we usually attend church but avoid the morning rush. That means no alarm clock for me. Instead, like many of you no doubt, I get to stumble out of bed late, splash cold water on my face, and head to the kitchen. With cartoons blaring in the background, I'm greeted by my dog, Julio, trying to hump my leg as I trip over the kids' scattered toys and find my wife in pajama bottoms and one of my old T-shirts. She hands me a cup of coffee and then, with a sweet smile, reminds me of everything I keep forgetting to do. That's my reality.

And that raises one more reason to write this book: so that eventually, many years into the future, my children will know about the journey I've taken and how it was shaped by the dreams of my parents and grandparents. In thinking about that possibility, I worry about all the lessons I have yet to teach them. Fortunately, we'll have time to do that. Besides, they'll want to make their own choices and learn their own lessons. Still, there is one I hope they'll discover from my takeaways. Simply: I'd have put more trust in God for my future back then, now, and tomorrow; I know He's got my back.

In the end, I wrote this book for *all* of us. For my fans—because I genuinely appreciate your loyal support all these years—and for everyone who has had a part in my story, and, again, for *me*, because I rarely slow down long enough to look in the rearview mirror of my life. Up until now, my focus has been in only one direction: forward.

Think of this as a long-overdue conversation, just between us. Thank you for coming along for the ride. For all my hesitation, I'm thrilled to get this all off my chest. My confessional booth is now open. As the map in the park was there to point out, without the past, without all its pain and glory, I wouldn't have arrived here, right where I am, blessed to be talking to you.

So this it: my story unfiltered, unplugged, and uncensored. *Vámonos.*

# CHAPTER 1

# STRAIGHT OUTTA CHULA

As the bird flies north over Mexico, he passes over the border town of Tijuana and then into the United States, and comes to the first stop before arriving in San Diego—the urban enclave of Chula Vista, California. Chula born and bred, I began life right there in a modest corner house on Paisley Street and grew up in that same neighborhood littered with single-level Monopoly-looking family dwellings. The scenery was a constant. Houses landscaped with rutted lawns, angry bushes, and snarled fencing. Streets cracked and potholed from the relentless Southern California sun. Chain-link fences, stray dogs, cars parked on the front lawn.

Chula Vista was my home, the world that raised me, and a part of my DNA. I loved it all—and still do.

We were a little more than three miles from the border with Mexico, just across from Tijuana. People would call my hometown "Chula Juana," because it's practically Mexico. We didn't cross the border; the border crossed us. As a result, living in Chula Vista—a predominantly Hispanic community—was a lot like living in Mexico. Even the signs were written in Spanish. There were taco stands and *mariscos* and *bodegas* on every block. Car radios driving through the center of Chula pumped mariachi music and the latest love songs sung by Mexican pop stars. And everybody spoke Spanish. My grandmother has been here—in this country—for fifty years and still doesn't speak English. That's how Mexican it was.

The name Chula Vista literally translates to "pretty view," and in Spanish slang becomes *Mama Chula* or *Papi Chulo*, meaning "sexy chick" or "sexy daddy." So I guess you could say I grew up in "Sexy Town." If that was to be part of my heritage, you would never have guessed it back when I was a baby. In fact, as my mom would often recall in the midst of family gatherings (in case anyone didn't know or had forgotten), "Mario was the fattest baby you've ever seen in your life!"

How fat was I? So fat, Mom would say, "I used to have to spread his skin apart to clean between the chubby rolls."

Other family members would soon start to comment, laughing and shaking their heads, as if they still couldn't believe how fat I was. Next thing I knew, somebody would bring out baby pictures to prove it.

And here's the truth: I really did look like one of those sharpei dogs. Or a Mexican Buddha. The reason, Mom would explain, was that I was breast-fed until after my first birthday and yet I would still eat everything in sight.

Luckily, I eventually outgrew my chubster stage. Even luckier was that I lived to tell the tale of what happened earlier, right after my birth, when by all the laws of modern medicine I was expected to die.

My mother tells this story even better than I do. Whenever the subject came up at a big get-together and she began to reminisce, you could hear a pin drop. Clearly, this was a traumatic memory for the relatives who went through it with my parents. At the time of my birth, my mom, Elvia Trasvina Lopez, and my dad, Mario Alberto Lopez, had been married for two and a half years. Both my mom and dad and their families came from the same city in

Mexico—Culiacán, the capital city of Sinaloa—although they didn't meet until they both lived here. They were also each around nineteen years old when they arrived, separately, of course, and legally—or, as we all used to joke in Chula Vista, at least I think it was legal. In any case, they were already bona fide U.S. citizens when they met in San Diego.

By that point, my dad had lived all over California before settling in the area and my mom had come directly to San Diego with her family. Without a doubt, Elvia must have had lots of young men pursuing her in those days. A beautiful woman with infectious energy that people would gravitate toward throughout her life, she had at one time worked as a model for runway and local fashion shows. Rather than being a girly girl, however, my mom was always just as comfortable in jeans and a T-shirt. Down-to-earth, charismatic, bright, and on the go, she also had this heart of gold and naturally took charge whenever family or friends in the neighborhood needed her help—like an angel. No wonder she caught my dad's eye.

As it so happened, Mom's brother, my *tío* Victor, knew my father before my parents met. Now, when it comes to machismo, my father wrote that book. He is a classic man's man, as old school as it gets. Always making sure he stays in shape, he's long been known for his physique: broad shouldered with big arms, a big chest, and big strong hands, and yet also as compact as a pit bull. Plus, he doesn't usually filter what he says or to whom—which, in his younger days, meant he didn't play by the rules and got himself into a bar fight or two. Well, that's how he met my uncle. Seems that they got into a fight over a girl they were both interested in. But because Dad knew how to shake hands after fists had flown, *Tío* Victor figured this guy was a gentleman and they became friends.

When my dad met the beautiful Elvia, he mentioned, coincidentally, that he knew her brother. A good icebreaker, I guess. Dad was quite the ladies' man, so much so that when he met my mom, he introduced himself as Richard Lopez. Why an alias? Because that way he would never get caught running around with another girl. Changing names was his system for staying straight. Once he realized Mom might be the one, he fessed up and told her his real name was Mario. She still didn't understand the point of the alias, but later on, when she did, Mom simply said, "Okay, well, you're always Richard to me." From then on, everybody called him Richard.

Elvia and Richard dated for a couple of years and settled into married life together before starting a family. When at last I was born on October 10, 1973, I was given the name Mario Lopez, which should have made me a junior, but for some reason my mom and dad opted not to give me the middle name of Alberto. That made me the only person of Mexican descent that I know who doesn't have at least one middle name. Nonetheless, I made a promising entrance, weighing in at eight and a half pounds, and was welcomed into life by all the grandparents, aunts, uncles, and older cousins who were on hand to celebrate the joyous occasion of my arrival. But then, to everyone's shock, almost overnight, I shrank to less than half my birth weight.

The problem, they later discovered, was that my stomach couldn't handle the milk. I'd vomit and have diarrhea and then become dehydrated. As soon as I showed signs of dehydration, my parents would rush me to the hospital and the doctors would use an IV of Pedialyte to quickly hydrate me. They did this over and over again, for a period of almost three months, without resolving the crisis. Before long, the doctors had to sit my anguished parents down to say there was nothing more they could do to prevent me from wasting away.

Whenever my mother told this story in a group, she would start to cry all over again, remembering how a doctor advised them, "You must prepare for the worst." The doctors thought I was going to die. It was not a matter of *if* but *when*.

A priest was called in to bless me and say a prayer—my last rites. My parents were beside themselves, understandably. But my father, stubborn to the bone, refused to accept the fate the doctors had handed down. With absolute conviction, he stated, "No! My son is NOT going to die."

Mario Alberto Lopez aka Richard had reason to believe the doctors could be wrong. In his younger days, before I was born, Dad had beaten a dire prognosis from medical experts. In that era, he worked in a machine shop where he hoisted heavy loads of material—over a hundred pounds at a time—all day long, moving the loads from one spot and then setting them on the milling machinery. After a while, in spite of his strength, the physical demands of his employment began to wreak havoc on his body. What kind of havoc? Really scary stuff. As my dad once told me, "My spine was completely crooked and I was in constant pain." Barely able to walk, he also couldn't sleep, no matter what medications they gave him. The doctors recommended an array of expensive tests and invasive procedures. But rather than accept that those were his only options, Dad agreed as a last resort to go with his dad, my grandfather Tata Lopez, to see a witch doctor, or *bruja*. She was located in an out-of-the-way place near Rosarito, Mexico. Upon seeing Dad and hearing of his ailments, she immediately went to work.

If anyone ever asked my father what she did exactly, he would only say, "Oh, she performed that Santeria black magic stuff you hear about." This seems to have involved cutting off a chicken's head and spraying the blood on him. And then some. Whatever the approach, it took all day and Dad walked out of there like a mummy, totally wrapped in bandages. During the healing process he had to bathe in seaweed from the ocean. As crazy as it sounds, it worked. She had managed to straighten out all of his bones. The witch doctor cured my dad.

This was my father's justification for taking the drastic action that he did when my condition worsened and the doctors deemed my case to be terminal. He and Mom had been through so much, constantly taking me back and forth from the hospital every time I became dehydrated. At his wit's end, my dad marched in and kidnapped me from the hospital—a last-ditch effort to save my life—and took me to be seen by the very same witch doctor who had saved him. Within an hour or so, he'd made it across the border, and in a candle-lit room filled with smoke the *bruja* made her mystery concoction. Eye of bat, wing of beetle, hair of dragon? Perhaps. Whatever the magic was, she mixed it with Pedialyte and *suero* (fermented milk like yogurt). She brewed it up, added goat's milk, and said to my dad, "Give him that." The concoction had Carnation evaporated milk in it—a quarter of the bottle—and the rest was mostly water.

It worked. No more vomiting or diarrhea. Digesting milk was no longer a problem. I was healed.

The same hospital that couldn't save me and was willing to almost leave me for dead also billed my parents for those same failed treatments. The bills made a huge stack about a foot high. The hospital charged my parents something like seventy grand— which was astronomical by 1973 standards. The hospital charges were for the care, not for the cure they didn't provide. The witch doctor cost six hundred dollars.

Within a few weeks after drinking the potion, I not only started putting on weight and rebuilding my strength, but my appetite spiked until it was off the charts. Making up for lost time, I was so insatiable, apparently, that I soon became that fat Mexican Buddha baby everybody in the family loved to joke about. According to reports, I just got fatter and fatter until I finally began to walk. And once I went bipedal, as my mom would say, "*Mijo*, all bets were off!"

Of course, she and my dad were thrilled with my full recovery and rapid transition into bruiser status. But that brought with it a new set of concerns. Like one night when I was just starting to motor around the house, wobbling from here to there. Mom and Dad, both seated on the couch, began to call my name at the same time, each opening up their arms, as if to see which parent I'd go to first. After toddling in one direction, I'd change at the last minute and wobble over to the other parent. Unable to make up my mind, I kept it up for a while, going back and forth until finally I fell face-first—*smack*—right onto the corner of the coffee table.

Mom began to wail, becoming hysterical at the sight of blood gushing from what turned out to be my broken nose, and then almost fainted, prompting my dad to rush both of us to the hospital—to get me stitches and to make sure she was going to be all right. In the aftermath, I was left with a pronounced Frankenstein scar on my nose between my eyes that you can still see if you look closely. Considering a multitude of other close calls in the years that followed, the scar is no big deal. Besides, it gives me character, or at least that's what the girls would say.

The broken nose hardly slowed me down. By the time I hit

preschool—in the period when our family grew to a total of four, thanks to the addition of my younger sister, Marissa, three years my junior—I was basically transformed into a young Speedy Gonzales. Living with boundless energy and very little fear, I may not have consciously recognized how lucky I was to be alive. But from as far back as I can remember, I had a vast appreciation for every experience that life had to offer and didn't want to miss a thing.

Whatever was happening at home, with our immediate family or with our larger extended family, at school or in the neighborhood, I wanted to be a part of it. Sometimes I wonder if the witch doctor didn't put in a little extra ingredient that made me into something of a ringleader or instigator. Or maybe this was just early training for my eventual hosting skills.

Who knows? What I do know is that I may have caught the performing bug as early as three years old, when, because of exposure to mariachi music, which my dad loved, I started singing Spanish songs and winning local competitions. It was also at age three that I started to read, something that came easily and that I'm sure my mother encouraged—and, allegedly, spurred my uncanny knack of being able to memorize what I've read or heard, even if I have no clue what any of it means. To the amazement of most adults, I could deliver word-perfect renditions of soaring mariachi ballads by the likes of Vicente Fernández, a Mexican icon. My dad couldn't resist bringing me with him to mariachi bars in Chula, where I would entertain him, his buddies, and whoever else was in the place. He would lift me up onto the bar and I would happily sing passionate love songs such as "Sangre Caliente," "La Ley del Monte," and "La Media Vuelta." This went on for years.

By no means were my early forays into mariachi music an indication to anyone in the family that entertainment could be my calling in life. Not by a long shot. The truth is, I was a hyper kid who could not sit still—what today would probably be seen as having some form of attention deficit issues—and so, to keep me from getting into serious trouble, Mom, in her infinite wisdom, had to devise a strategic plan of action. Her first move? Enrolling me in dance class at age three. It took me many years before I figured out the method to the madness.

Back in the day—I'm talking about Chula Vista of the 1970s, up until I was six or seven years old—I assumed everybody around me was Mexican too. I thought everybody spoke Spanish, ate tacos, liked Chihuahuas (for want of a better stereotype), and had a last name that ended with z—Gonzalez, Fernandez . . . Lopez. And so on. This was only natural. When you're a kid, the world outside your window is the world. So, of course, I concluded that everyone was just like me. Soon enough, I would learn that wasn't true at all.

Yes, much of the population of Chula was Mexican, but we also were home to a mix of other Hispanics and fellow immigrant families, not to mention a few white people—the "salt" sprinkled on the top of the colorful, multicultural melting pot in which we, Latinos, were the majority. The diversity had to do with the nearby navy base in San Diego, which attracted all types and nationalities to the area. Chula Vista had a strong Filipino community, a black community, even a Samoan community. Eventually, once I started meeting people from different backgrounds, I gained a much broader worldview. The differences, in my opinion, were cool. Not only did I become extremely accepting of others who weren't like me, but I genuinely enjoyed getting to know how those differences shaped them—their race, culture, food, music, lifestyle, you name it. That inclusive attitude is part of the world that shaped my sensibilities and is an aspect of what makes San Diego so beautiful.

The atmosphere of inclusion is probably also what allowed me, a border-town kid, to grow up feeling that my childhood was really all-American—in the way that I felt connected to fellow citizens, that this was my country and we all belonged. Those patriotic, traditional values were prevalent in Chula Vista, and important to my upbringing. Once my schooling started, weirdly, it was almost like growing up in the fifties—kids' parties, school dances, local hangouts, football rallies, prom, and constant family involvement. Kind of like a Latino-themed *Happy Days*.

Then again, Chula neighborhoods like mine were tough, especially back in the 1970s and '80s. As a border town, we had criminal elements associated with drug smuggling and hard-core gangs that added to dangers for everyone. We were, after all, the barrio—the inner city that could be even tougher than in comparable blue-collar neighborhoods of Boston or Chicago. Like those being raised in urban areas, we too weren't free to roam in the woods and run around building forts, making slingshots and bows and arrows, or learning to hunt and fish. Instead, in Chula Vista we played football in the streets, dueled each other in mud- and rock-throwing contests, and, more or less, lived on our bikes.

The good news from this mix of influences was that Chula offered an education in itself—a way to appreciate my heritage, to enjoy a normal childhood in a hardworking middle-class community with all-American values, and to develop the street smarts that living in a tough neighborhood demands. Of course, the foundation for all these lessons came from growing up among the colorful cast of characters who were members of my extended family on both the Lopez and Trasvina sides.

Whenever there was any excuse for a get-together, the word

would go out and next thing we knew all the relatives would converge either at our house on Paisley Street or, most of the time, over at the home of my maternal grandmother, Nana Trasvina. A matriarch of our family, Nana probably had the strongest influence on me during my childhood, other than that of my parents. She was a true sweetheart, loved everybody unconditionally, and, as a devout Catholic, lived her faith by example, going to church daily at six a.m. Nana always had on an apron because with all of us congregating so often at her house, she was always cooking. In fact, I never saw her when she wasn't in the kitchen. And I never saw her when she wasn't in a beautiful mood.

Nana's solution to a household full of rambunctious kids was to insist we go play outside. Her belief that fresh air and exercise were important was what later inspired my children's book, *Mud Tacos*. The story captures the essence of my early childhood, back when kids had to use their imaginations, back before computers and iPads. All of us kids in the neighborhood would team up and make mud tacos—mud, leaves, and worms. Beef, taco, and cheese. We'd set up our little kitchen outside and make up plates full of mud tacos to share with the family.

In hindsight, I'm amazed that when it came to our gatherings we all could fit inside Nana's house or ours. Besides our family of four—Mom, Dad, Marissa (pronounced *Ma-ree-sa*), and me—the lineages included Mom's five brothers and five sisters along with their kids, and Dad's four brothers and four sisters as well as their kids. Mom was the oldest girl. And Dad was the oldest, period. He always seemed older than fire and dirt.

All of my cousins lived across the street, around the corner, or within walking distance. Louie and Gabe lived across the street, Alex and Victor and Ralphie lived around the corner, and all of my mom's family—everybody—lived within a couple of miles of each other. The saying *"Mi casa es su casa"* really applied, no matter where we gathered, as did the phrase "The more the merrier." Man, did I love those times, so much so that even though I'm no longer in Chula Vista, my house in LA is still ground zero for over-flowing get-togethers.

Having a tight-knit group of male cousins helped make up for my lack of brothers. One of my absolute favorites was my *primo* Louie. On the Lopez side, he was the son of my father's younger brother, the oldest of three boys, and a good-looking, all-around great kid. With a ready smile, he had that gift of lighting up a room when he walked into it—not in a boisterous way, more like the glow of a warm candle. Unbeknownst to the family, he knew he was gay early in his teens but didn't come out until much later, during a turbulent period for him after he had abruptly left Chula Vista. After the fact, I was upset that he felt he had to keep the reality of who he was and whom he loved a secret from the family, who would have accepted him no matter what. His story, as it later unfolded, would impact all of us, as would that of my cousin and godson Chico.

There were times as I approached adolescence when I naturally sought out the counsel of my older male cousins to help give me insights on stuff like girls and other worldly matters—sometimes at my own peril. Meanwhile, my younger cousins were like younger brothers for whom I tried to set a good example, though not always successfully. Ironically, although Marissa is three years younger than me, she's about a hundred years older than me in terms of maturity. Marissa does not mess around. Direct and focused, she has the rep in the family for being that person who will tell you the way it is. And tough? She was definitely braver than me, pushing the envelope with Mom and Dad much more than I did.

As different as my sister and I could sometimes be, we both

loved our family gatherings and enjoyed hearing the stories that would inevitably come to light after a few *cervezas* at a family get-together.

"Oh, and what about the time you . . ." someone would start, bringing up a story everybody had heard over and over, and the next thing we knew the entertainment would begin. The music would quiet down and us kids would draw in close, listening wide-eyed as the other person would say, "No, that wasn't me. You must be thinking of somebody else. Here's what really happened."

Then came the tales of what it was like back when our parents and aunts and uncles were growing up in Sinaloa—what's now known as the drug capital of Mexico. Despite its dark side, Sinaloa has some of the most beautiful countryside and beaches you've ever seen and is also known all over Mexico for its beautiful people. From the reputation we heard it had, it seemed that life there was like being in the middle of the Wild, Wild West of Mexico—whether or not you had any contact with the Sinaloa cartel, notorious for having in its ranks the most powerful and dangerous druglords, male and female.

Though I never found out the details, our family in Culiacán may have included relatives high up on the cartel food chain. Whenever I asked, though, I'd get one of those answers like, "If we tell you, we have to kill you."

"How bad could the drug gangs be?" I asked my dad once.

"They're serious" was all he would say. Apparently, the Mexican cartels were nothing like your average "sell on the corner" ringleaders or the "made men" like in *The Sopranos*. They were Colombian serious. Pablo Escobar serious.

That gave me some perspective, but I never got the full story about whether or not Dad at one point was brought briefly into the family end of that business. I figure he couldn't have been in too deep, because he's still alive. Nobody else in our extended group of family members was involved, for sure. If anyone was connected, though, Dad was probably the only one who had the balls, or the insanity, for that kind of thing.

Those weren't the stories discussed in family gatherings, but you never knew what someone might decide to bring up. There was also constant joking and catching up on the latest news and gossip—Trasvina does mean "through the grapevine"—and food and drink, needless to say, along with music, sometimes live, and always dancing.

Oh, and gambling. We gambled on every card game we could. As a fierce competitor ever since I can remember, I was really into a game called acey-deucey—and still am. It's simple. You're dealt two cards out in front of you, faceup. Then you bet on the next card being a value between those two cards. Say you bet a buck. If the third card is between your first two cards, you win the dollar. If it's not, you lose the dollar. If it has the same value as either of your first two cards, you pay double. So the pot would get huge.

Basically, acey-deucey is a game of luck. It's all in the deal of the cards. You can decide not to bet, if you aren't feeling lucky. But otherwise your fate is all up to chance. Maddening to everyone else, I was often lucky with cards and in other respects.

But in the family I come from, leaving anything up to chance in life was not going to cut it. Not with Mom and her master plan to keep me *out* of trouble. The problem wasn't just that I was a nonstop bundle of energy who could get into trouble faster than the average kid. The complicating factor by 1980, when I turned seven years old, was the increase of gang activity in Chula Vista, and it seemed easy for many kids to get caught up in that life and all the dealings that came with it. Some of my *primos* and other relatives got caught up and never could get out.

My mom was a genius. Her whole philosophy was: if I can keep Mario as busy as possible, he won't have time to get into trouble. And it worked, mostly because I didn't want to disappoint her, knowing how much she loved and adored me. She, like everyone in her family, was always affectionate. She told me that she loved me every single day, and she kissed me every day, and that's just the way I am.

Mom's plan was the key not just to keeping me out of trouble but, moreover, to my becoming who I am today.

The cardinal sin of all sins in our household was laziness. My parents each had their own turbocharged version of a work ethic that melded into one. And ultimately I must have inherited the hard-work gene from both my parents. Clearly, I had no choice. There wasn't a moment when I got to just be lazy.

To their lasting credit, Elvia and Richard Lopez led by example. My mom, in addition to working full-time as an operator with the phone company, was a force of nature in overseeing concerns for the whole extended family, not to mention in raising two kids. Dad was either at work or out in the garage fixing up old cars or he was busy outside doing yard work or whatever other manly projects he could undertake to be productive.

"Mario, what are you doing?" Dad asked every time he happened to catch me kicking back and watching a little TV.

"I finished my homework . . ." I'd begin, but before I could finish, he'd send me out to help in the yard or do whatever else he could think up that needed doing.

Mom's chore of choice was to have me vacuum, though I honestly didn't mind. I liked vacuuming in very straight lines, so when I was done there was a cool pattern left on the rug. If you have to do it, why not make it fun?

In teaching us to be responsible for chores, I don't think my parents necessarily meant for work and fun to be synonymous. Along with the concept of responsibility came a message of toughness: that hard work might require sacrifice and guts. The lesson was that you worked hard to take care of your family, whatever it entailed.

No question that Dad was toughness personified, working many different jobs through the years, even though he was awfully mysterious about what exactly they were. One thing was evident: he didn't leave in the morning dressed in a suit and swinging a briefcase. For a while he ran a little landscaping business, and then, when I was around thirteen or so, he got his first real steady job working for the city as a machinist. Later, he worked for the street department, setting up sobriety checkpoints, driving big trucks. In between, odd jobs based on his many talents filled in the gaps.

My dad was entrepreneurial in an old-school way, going the extra mile to help improve our lifestyle. He drove an older but cherried-out Cadillac and magically restored vintage cars that had been left on the junk heap. Money didn't just appear by itself, but I can remember how he enjoyed counting stacks of cash around the house—separating the singles, tens, and twenties into orderly piles. He didn't try to hide it. Why would he? We all knew enough not to ask stupid questions. After he was done counting, he put the money in his pockets, in bags, in the dresser.

The reward to my sister and me for all this hard work was our Sunday drive to Tijuana for authentic *mariscos*, Mexican seafood. Before the attacks of September 11, 2001, the border patrol rarely hassled anyone with American license plates upon entering Mexico or even upon returning. We'd spend the day shopping around in Tijuana, then feast on delicious crab, lobsters, fish, shrimp, spicy yellow rice, and turtle (not illegal back then), eat until we were stuffed, and after dinner turn around and come right back to the States.

Marissa and I were typical kids—we didn't pay much attention to what our parents were doing. But around the age of ten, I recall a few occasions when I couldn't help but notice that after we came back from across the border and happened to be driving along a deserted stretch of road, Dad pulled over onto a gravel shoulder and got out of the car. My eyes followed him as far as I could as he went behind the car and opened the trunk, as if he was just checking something out. Well, from what I could gather, it wasn't something—it was someone. A few someones. Like four or five. Or that's what I thought when I saw that many people who seemed to have come out of nowhere suddenly make a run for it and disappear into the brush. In shock, I sat there slack-jawed, wondering how the hell they'd gotten in the trunk, how long they'd been riding in there, whether they could even breathe. Those people had to be crazy to do that, or so I thought. But I never asked my dad about it. It was *understood* that he was in charge and knew what he was doing.

There were a couple of other such instances, I think, though again I can't be sure. I also have a vague memory of my dad bringing over birds—exotic birds—right in the trunk of that Cadillac. And who knows what else? He didn't tell and I never asked.

Like I said, memory has clouded the details for me. The fact was, you heard about rides across the border like that during the very rough Mexican economy in the eighties, a time when undocumented workers were in high demand in this country.

Whether or not we did have extra cargo in other instances, you wouldn't have guessed by my dad's demeanor when we came back across the border, as I kind of remember on one occasion, and the customs officer asked, "Citizenship?"

With nerves of steel, my dad answered, "American citizen." That could have been iffy; I don't know.

The officer proceeded, "What are you bringing back?"

"Oh, nothing, just my two kids. We went to get something to eat."

That was all. Who could have pulled that off if there was anything suspicious in the trunk? Nobody. Well, maybe nobody. After that, the way to avoid further scrutiny would have been to drive on past Chula Vista, on into the outskirts of Dana Point, at the far northern border of the San Diego county line. But I wouldn't know anything about that.

What I did know was that Dad took care of us and did what he had to do to provide. Looking back, I also think that Dad—given the kind of opportunities that I would later enjoy—could have been a very good actor, even a movie star. He had the best style, rocking the seventies gear like John Travolta in *Saturday Night Fever*, dressed in the low-button shirts and flared pants, like he was getting ready to go hit the dance floor. Dad was the kind of guy who could wear two-dollar cologne and smell like a million bucks. His signature scent? Jovan Musk. It came in an orange cologne bottle and smelled fantastic on him. I've been with him countless times when women would come over and ask, "Excuse me, what are you wearing?"

International man of mystery that he was, my dad subscribed completely to Mom's master plan for keeping me busy and out of trouble, such as when she signed me up to spend my afternoons at the local Boys Club. Though I had no choice in the matter, I understood that it was a place to keep me safe and off the streets. It wouldn't take long for me to throw myself in all they had to offer, especially wrestling. Today the organization is called the Boys and Girls Clubs of America, but back then it was just the Boys Clubs of America. No girls allowed. Wrestling was a godsend, just what Mom had been hoping to find for me, and so too was the Boys Club.

Because both Mom and Dad worked full-time, that meant that my weekdays were carefully structured—starting with school, then with dance class and wrestling and the other after-school activities as they were added for me and Marissa, and then ending up at Nana's house. As she and my grandfather spoke only Spanish, that was actually my first language, and by conversing with them as I was growing up, I was able to remain fluent. I loved our home away from home with Nana and Tata. It was like having another set of parents, except they let me get away with a lot more.

Nana Trasvina, deeply religious, made sure that we were raised with strong connections to the Catholic Church. Without question, faith would become a staple in my life as it was for most of my family. In my view, there is a connection between hard work and the faith needed not to give up even during tough times. The rituals of religion, however, were more complicated to me, especially at a young age. Certainly, the Chula Vista community of Catholic Latinos was very religious, and I grew up surrounded by crosses and Bibles and verse and prayer. Even though my father didn't go to church regularly and Marissa only went intermittently, I attended Mass on most weekends mainly because my mom did. She, Nana, and I would go together. Again, in my mother's eyes, anything to keep Mario busy was a no-brainer—even though it was brutal having to sit still for that long and not lose my mind.

As an adult now, church has become a place of solace for me, one of the few places where I can go to be alone and with my thoughts. Where I can recharge. And I like being Catholic—from the serenity and the culture of the religion to the respect it inspires, to the history and the teachings of charity and giving. In the crazy chaos of life these days, it's a pause in which to disconnect and become centered, a way to start every week fresh all over again. I love the art associated with Catholicism and have a beautiful collection of vintage crosses that today hang on the walls of my house.

But before I matured enough to appreciate my time in church, I struggled with some basic rituals during my Communion classes. It made no sense to me that the bread they use for the Communion wafer, which symbolizes the body of Christ, had to taste horrible. One of the first times I had to try a wafer in catechism class, I whispered to the kid next to me, "Tastes like the nuns took cardboard from a graham cracker box and rolled it in mothballs!"

At seven years old, I was showing signs of having a gift of gab. The other kid cracked up but luckily I didn't get into trouble with the SWAT team of nuns. Emboldened, I came up with a way to avoid eating the wafers. Whenever it came time, I'd put the wafer on my tongue, chew it a little, then secretly turn, spit it out into my hand, and hide it between the Bibles in the back of the pew seats. Worked like a charm. At first. Until one of the younger nuns caught me spitting it out and gave me a strong scolding. Yet that wasn't enough to stop me from hiding chewed-up Communion wafers between the Bibles. I just couldn't gum down the dry cracker and swallow it. But eventually my luck ran out, and I was caught once again. The nuns finally complained to my parents about my ongoing misdeeds.

"Mario, I'm so disappointed," Mom began when she sat me down. "Spitting out the Holy Communion is a sin. It's disrespectful to the Church. You should know better!" She was so upset that Dad got upset.

I had no defense. That perfect storm of indiscretions meant I had to be spanked. If the nuns would have just put jelly on the holy wafer for kids, I could have saved myself from Dad's belt. When it came to discipline, my dad maintained a fairness policy. If I deserved punishment, he would not hesitate to dole it out. But he was never unnecessarily rough. Rather, he primarily used his dominating presence to keep us in line, ruling with intimidation, in a deep bellowing voice; the fear didn't come from his physical strength but his position as my father. He did have his pet peeves. Like how I made a clicking noise with my tongue and teeth whenever he told me to do something. "Don't suck on your teeth," he'd say and give me a glance that meant that I was not living in a democratic household and this was not open to negotiation.

My dad didn't need to do much to make a point. If I had a short fuse and was acting out, all he had to say was, "Mario. *Ven aquí.*" One look and I knew I'd better quit. If I defied him or didn't listen, well, usually, that was cause for the belt. But he never slapped me with his hands. Thank God, because if he had, he would have laid me out.

Whenever Dad unleashed the belt, the trick was to cry as soon as possible. The sooner you started crying, the less of a whopping. It wouldn't totally save me from all pain, but it would speed things along. In time, I learned to let my thespian skills take over.

Mom was another story. As the main disciplinarian in the household, she was immune to my theatrics and I feared her more than I did my father. Mom used a shoe as her weapon of choice, although she was skilled at wielding the belt too—she liked to mix it up. Heaven forbid her discipline technique should become mundane.

Angelic as she is, Mom's toughness would come out with others whenever certain lines were crossed. Talk about a mama bear protecting her cubs. Relatives used to say, "Don't mess with Elvia's kids, because she'll get nasty."

I saw a glimmer of that after an incident at the first Catholic school I attended, Covenant Christian School. Let me just note that neither my mom nor dad expected the school to be responsible for teaching their kids discipline. They did expect us to be diligent students. At the four different elementary schools I would attend, I was a very good student, for the most part. One reason for that was because I always went to summer school—yet another aspect of keeping me active. The summer programs were held at different schools every year and I was exposed to a variety of teaching methods. Unfortunately, back in the second grade at Covenant Christian School, the teaching methods included the nuns' apparent fondness for paddling.

Mom heard one too many reports of me getting paddled. "That's it," she told my dad. "We're pulling him out." She refused to let anybody hit her child. In fact, when she came to pull me out of the school for good, I heard her explain to the staff, "If anybody's going to hit my kid, it's going to be me."

The first time I ever stepped foot in our local Boys Club, I felt at home. The sense of belonging was almost instantaneous. Even at seven years old, I could see that the Boys Club was not just a place where busy parents sent their kids (like me) to keep them off the streets, but it was also a haven for children who had no parents to speak of. We had every kind of activity to choose from. Besides the wrestling that I dove into—like a fish to water—we played football and most ball sports, along with pool and air hockey and all kinds of games that everyone could play. The adults leading the program were former inner-city kids who knew all too well of the pitfalls for anyone growing up in the barrio.

My wrestling coaches were the real deal. We had one resident coach whose breath reeked of alcohol and, because of his drinking problem, didn't last. But Coach Walt Mikowachek was fantastic and I'll never forget him. A Polish guy, he was just full of life and a great all-around human being, probably the first person outside of our family I really respected. Coach Walt cared about all of us and made us feel important. He invariably showed interest in what and how I was doing, exemplifying what it meant to be a mentor. Sometimes, you just have to be there for a kid and that's more than enough. Any sort of consistency in a young person's life means a lot. Some mentors at the Boys Club gave kids rides home at the end of the day, or others would get them a new pair of shoes—which could mean everything in the world to those kids who didn't have shoes at all.

As I went further into wrestling, my dad—who was never super demonstrative with his affections—showed his support in his own subdued way, showing up when I was competing and standing right on the corner of the mat. But I knew he was proud and I appreciated when every now and then I heard him say, "C'mon, *mijo!*" I didn't need much egging on, as I was naturally competitive and pushed myself all the time, even when the stakes didn't seem high. True, some of my dad's cool rubbed off on me in other ways, but part of my competitive streak probably came more from Mom. My sister got some of that too, but more than anything Marissa really inherited our mother's great compassion for others and her sense of responsibility.

My dad was more of a jokester most of the time than outright competitive. Or he'd pretend something was serious when it wasn't—like when he challenged me to play this stupid arm wrestling game, the one where two people lock their middle fingers together and twist in opposite directions.

Don't try this at home, but here's the drill: You stick out your middle finger, the other person sticks out theirs, you lock them together, and both of you make a fist with that same hand. Now both people are knuckle-to-knuckle with their middle fingers locked together. One guy twists to the right and the other guy twists to the left. The person who can't stand the pain and lets go first is the loser. Dad broke his finger a few times playing that game with adults, but that's because he's not a guy who gives up easily, and because in those instances he was at a party after drinking a few.

Did I mention my dad could outdrink anyone? That's what they did back then. He could hold his liquor like nobody. Well, except for one time when he and Mom were hosting a house party and I happened to see him quietly head outside to throw up near the garden hose. To my shock, afterward he rinsed out his mouth with the hose, went right back inside, and continued to drink. Other than that time, I never thought he had a problem—that is, until I got older and I would notice how much he could knock back. A whole bottle of Bacardi 151 like it was nothing. Yet he was never sloppy. Never. That said, I might have decided at a certain point when I was growing up that *some* moderation when it came to alcohol could be a good way to go.

As for moderation with wrestling, that never crossed my mind. Our practice at the Boys Club was fun, but it also involved serious training and I found that I thrived with the challenge. We did single-leg takedowns, fireman carries, head and arm maneuvers during which you'd be on top and try to work the ground control. We did half-Nelsons and guillotines, as well as pinning techniques, where you would try to pin your opponent so that both shoulder blades touched the ground for at least a second, until you heard the slap on the mat from the ref. When you got a pin, that was like a knockout. There is nothing like hearing the sound of the slap on the mat when the pin is yours.

"Mario, where did you get that move?" Coach Walt would ask whenever he spotted me horsing around before or after practice, especially if I was trying out some outlandish wrestling maneuver that I'd seen on TV. These moves would never be allowed in practice, but we all attempted to try them out on each other. If I liked what I saw, I would mess around and test out the possibilities on the next unsuspecting kid I was set to spar. None of those intricately choreographed moves that you'd see on WWF would ever work in a real contest, but they looked so good, we all attempted to incorporate elements of them.

My favorite move for a time was the "suplex." When I saw it on WWF, I knew before practice that I had to spring a hard-core move like that on my next sparring partner, Hector Cruz. The suplex starts as you grab your opponent and put your arm around his head—like a headlock, but from the front, a rear naked choke. You grab him in a headlock and put your other arm behind his head. Then you grab him by his pants, jump up, go backward, and slam him down on the mat. Almost like a back flip. Now, on TV the mats are probably expensive and have more padding. But most mats in youth wrestling are not that thick, only about two and a half inches at most. So when I went for the suplex move and had him by the neck, I was aware enough to try to soften his landing when I threw him backward over my shoulder and jammed him onto the floor. *Bam!*

Hector definitely got the wind knocked out of him that time, although it could have been worse. After coming close to really doing damage, I backed off of doing the suplex. Another move I'll never do again is the figure-four leg lock, especially after the kid sprained his knee. There's no real way to get out of that move unless you have a Taser or a knife.

I should emphasize that back in my early wrestling years not only did we all attempt some of these ridiculous moves, but we all had the wind knocked out of us or got dizzy enough to see stars. Later on, when I got to high school and competed at meets, I would become known as a vicious competitor on the wrestling mats, combining my training with a high level of intensity. That will to win was just part of who I was, and, well, accidents did happen—for example, the times I broke one opponent's shoulder, or another's collarbone. There was one instance when I suffered a broken right ankle, forcing me to wear a cast. Impatient to get back into competition, I cut off the cast myself and had my coach tape up my foot and ankle. But in my next meet against a rival high school, my opponent zoned in on my right foot and kept coming at it so intentionally, I not so accidentally warned him in the clinch, "Lay off or I will jack you up." The next series of moves proved he wasn't going to lay off my ankle, so I proceeded to take him down with a move he didn't see coming—a move that audibly broke his arm.

Could all of this explain why friends nowadays will not get into any sort of ring or on any sort of mat with me? Even though I got the reputation for going too hard and playing too rough during my younger days, friends apparently still worry that as soon as I step inside the ring, I become the wrestler—or, as my later interests took me, the boxer. Maybe they're right. Even back in my Boys Club wrestling days or just fooling around with friends, the odds increased for someone getting hurt. It happened so often that as soon as someone was injured, my parents instantly thought, "Mario wrestling . . ."

The truism that your reputation almost always precedes you, even when you're innocent, is one of those lessons that I discovered. A case in point later on was the tree-climbing episode that happened one afternoon when I was hanging out with my pal James Garcia and my parents were not home—they might have been visiting across the street at my uncle's house. The tree in question in our backyard offered ideal tree-climbing practice: a tall, smooth trunk with thick, forked branches that I loved to climb really high. The way to get to the very top required one particular death-defying crux move—a big jump from one branch to another, Tarzan-style.

Fearless in a prone-for-trouble way, I had the benefit of agility honed in wrestling, so this was no big deal, and James figured if I was going to climb, so would he. Why not? Going up ahead of him, I demonstrated the flying squirrel move—jumped and grabbed the high branch, scampering close to the trunk to make room for James to follow suit. Oh, he jumped all right, but as he went to grab for the branch—I watched it unfold as in slow motion—he missed the branch and nearly swan-dived as he fell to the ground with a *thud* and a *crack*.

"Please, God," I started to pray as I descended from the tree at record speed. "Don't let him be hurt." How bad was it? Well, let me put it this way: that was the first time I witnessed a bone break through the skin. It protruded through the inside of his forearm, broken for sure.

When I ran inside to call 911—the first time I ever had to

make an emergency call myself—the operator assumed that I'd broken James's arm. What? Who had she been talking to?

She kept repeating, "Now tell me again—how did you break your friend's arm?" and I kept repeating, "I didn't break his arm—he fell out of a tree!"

How she came to that assumption, I never knew.

When my parents came home a short time later, before I could tell them the story, the first thing my dad said was, "Mario, how many times do we have to tell you to stop the WWF wrestling moves?"

"No, Dad, we weren't wrestling. He fell out of the tree!"

He and Mom both looked at each other as though I had to be kidding.

Eventually, James did convince my parents that it wasn't my fault and had nothing to do with wrestling. He survived, thank God, though not without a significant scar from the fall—and from the operation he had to have to set things right again.


"**D**ance class?"

That, apparently, had been my only reaction when I was three years old after Mom first enrolled me in the most basic of all dance classes. Who was I to question my mother? As time went on, it became more obvious that because Mom loved to dance she wanted me to learn. And with her grand design to keep me busy and out of trouble she may have chosen dance as an activity that might balance out my more rambunctious side.

Whatever her intention, as the years of elementary school went by I continued to be enough of a mama's boy not to object to dance class. And so I became the only dancing wrestler I knew. My classes were in jazz and tap at All That Jazz, a dance studio in

Chula Vista. All That Jazz was exactly what you would imagine when you think of a dance studio in a border town like Chula in the early eighties: a simple little studio in the middle of a strip mall.

Every time I started a new series of classes, I'd walk in and enter a familiar scene: parents hovering over their little girls as they waited for class to begin—and then there was me and my mom. Most of the time, I was the only boy in the class. Was I embarrassed about that? Yep. But I stuck it out because I couldn't let Mom down. Even knowing that the boys at school would tease me, I couldn't bear the thought of making my mother sad or, worse, breaking her heart. She was into dancing!

At about nine years old or so, I remember no longer feeling as awkward about being the only boy in class—especially now that I was beginning to notice girls more. It started to dawn on me that I was learning to move well and that girls liked that. Then I really embraced dance. Other boys would come in every now and then, but they'd always quit and I'd continue to rule the roost.

My ambivalence about dance class subsided even more whenever All That Jazz held contests and recitals. The theatrics were kind of exciting and so was the idea of competing for awards. Mom was in heaven, throwing herself into all the preparations as if she had found her true calling. All of sudden, as dress rehearsals loomed, I became her little toy—a living, breathing action figure she could dress up however she wanted. She'd make all of my costumes and take care of every detail until I looked like I was on some early version of *Toddlers & Tiaras*. Mom's competitive streak really came out at these times. If the girl dancers were going to be made up by their mothers, then she was going to give me makeup too. That's right: Mom brushed my cheeks with blush and costumed me in boy versions of sequined outfits for all the performances that she could. My repertoire in tap and jazz had me dancing to every over-the-top hit song of the eighties, including "Disco Duck" and John Travolta's performance of "You're the One That I Want." Or then there was classic rock and roll with choreography to the likes of Elvis's "All Shook Up." The first award I won from my studio was for a dance I did to "Wanna Be Startin' Somethin'" by Michael Jackson—a memorable experience that could well have shaped my eventual path in entertainment.

Maybe not. What I do know as an adult is that all I have to do is hear the intro to anything by Michael Jackson—like "Off the Wall" and "P.Y.T. (Pretty Young Thing)"—and in a flash the music takes me back to all the dance competitions in those years. MJ was my favorite and still is. For me, it's impossible to listen to any Michael Jackson hit and not get up and dance. To this day, I still know the choreography of every one of his music videos, mainly because I incorporated all those routines into my own dance recitals and competitions.

As much as I would never have admitted it then, dancing was a perfect outlet for me—a way for me to channel my excess energy like nothing else ever had. And nobody got injured in the process.

My complaints didn't end immediately. I mean, what cool boy ever took a dance class? But the happier that my dancing made Mom and the more I realized I had a knack for it, the more I accepted that dance was a part of who I was. Even before lessons, I could always move and groove, and loved dancing around the house. And now I loved dance class. At age ten, I was just beginning to understand how being the only guy in class with all girls certainly couldn't hurt. Well, as it became apparent later, the only straight guy anyway, which was just as good. But I eventually saw that any activity where you're the only guy in a room of attractive females wearing tiny little outfits was not a bad thing.

To my surprise, dancing even helped me with balance, agility, and grace in sports. It complemented all the other guy stuff I was doing. As soon as I realized that, I developed a genuine love for dancing, a love that has never died. That doesn't mean I wasn't teased. "Mama's boy" didn't bother me so much, because it was sort of true. "Sissy" was not cool, but I dealt with it. But when a kid called me "fag" one day, it was enough already—on top of the menacing way he said it—and that really bothered me. I didn't want to say anything back because I was a nice guy and generally not confrontational. But I could only take so much before it was time to stand up for myself and for anyone who got called names of any kind.

As I thought about how to respond, I explained to Mom that I didn't want to get into trouble but that I had to defend myself.

Mom was very clear about how she felt. *"Mijo,"* she said, "if this guy or some other guy picks on you like this and you don't kick his butt, I'm gonna kick *your* butt."

I'll never forget the intense look in her eyes. I nodded but hesitated. Did she really mean that?

My mom continued: "I'm not going to fight your battles for you. You do what you have to do." She then offered that when the school day was over, she would pick me up a couple of blocks away from the usual spot. What did she suggest? She went on, "I want you to wait for him after school. You tell him what the deal is. And if he doesn't apologize, then you kick his butt."

When the kid walked out of school the next day, I was waiting for him. He looked like a badass, cocky and cool in dark jeans, a long-sleeved T-shirt, and a pair of Vans. After I strode right up to him, I locked in on his eyes and said, "Hey, you know what, man?"

"What?"

As I got closer to him and started to let him know that he needed to leave me alone, he took a step toward me and soon we were talking back and forth at one another. With his short fuse, I didn't need to say much to trigger it. Finally he closed in on me, and instead of just walking away or ignoring him, a switch flipped and I went into full-on wrestling mode. Unless you're trained, you could never win a fight against a practiced wrestler. In no time, I got him in a double-leg takedown. And then he was just on the ground. *Boom*. I started pounding him. After a minute or two, he said, "All right, all right."

As planned, my mom picked me up a couple of blocks away. We passed the kid as he was limping his way down the street and Mom pulled up next to him, rolled down the car window, and yelled, "You deserved it!"

You have to love a badass mom. For sure, she preferred for me to resolve conflicts by keeping my cool. But Mom also didn't want any wimps in the family. She wouldn't stand for it. Nor could she tolerate it when her kids acted indifferent or wishy-washy.

On the other side of the spectrum, I had to learn restraint. Once I became a good wrestler, I couldn't fight with anyone just because I felt like it. It wasn't the right thing to do if they didn't have the training I did. But that wasn't a problem as far as the teasing went. Once I handled myself with that particular kid, I was set. Word travels fast in school and after that day everybody was cool with me. Dancer or not, no one called me names again. I could have danced in the middle of the cafeteria and not heard a single word about it.

That rite of passage was a golden ticket to the future. I learned that if you're going to be a dancer, or an actor, you're going to get teased. That's just how it is. The lesson is just to let those idiots say what they want and ignore them the best you can. Stand up to the ones you can't ignore. And, as I truly am today, be grateful for the kids who were mean—they toughened me up for some of the harsh realities I'd encounter later in showbiz.

All in all, as I look back on the preparation for life that I was given growing up in my family and in Chula Vista, I'm grateful to everyone and for everything that happened. Do I have any regrets? None really. Except, well, I would have spent more time with my grandparents, both sets of them. You have to love family while you have family. If I could go back, just once, I'd memorize the moments and never let them go.

CHAPTER 2

# CHILD ACTOR

As if it was yesterday, I still remember the moment when the trajectory of my life suddenly changed course—even if I had no idea at the time. Ten years old, I was backstage, standing in the wings of the massive auditorium at Grossmont High School in El Cajon, California, where I was waiting for the start of a recital to include All That Jazz and many of the other dance studios from across the region. At this big annual competition, the different studios were there to compete for what to me was some cheesy old trophy. But judging by the buzz backstage, as dance teachers and stage moms gave last-minute instructions to nervous dancers, you would have thought we were opening at Carnegie Hall.

Just before Mom left to take her seat in the auditorium, she double-checked my costume and the full makeup I had to wear for this show. After giving me a thumbs-up, she was starting to leave the backstage area when we both overheard a group of mothers next to us telling their daughters that there were a lot of dance industry talent scouts out in the audience. One of the moms said in a loud whisper, "I heard that Christine Guerrero, a talent agent, is here!"

Apparently, the San Diego–based agent had shown up to scout possible new talent to add to her roster. She represented children and young models and actors, securing bookings that were mostly small-scale local commercials and locally sponsored print ads. The moms next to us were all excited. Christine Guerrero, another mom explained, was there to see if any of the girls competing in the recital had what it takes.

This was not the first time that I had overheard dance parents telling their children that they had to start auditioning for jobs like dance shows—and if they were lucky, they might break into commercials and print modeling, and then maybe book something really big and earn a lot of money. And I had also noticed many a starry-eyed dancer who couldn't help tugging on a mom's sleeve, begging to be on TV or in the movies. Yet the concept was foreign to me.

Did I have dreams of the future at that time? Well, between us . . . yep, I did. But not as a child actor; not that young. My dream was to be a professional wrestler. I loved Hulk Hogan and the WWF, Roddy "Rowdy" Piper, Brutus "The Barber" Beefcake, Tito Santana. The appeal was about what they did and their larger-than-life personas—not about being on TV.

My mom had never shown an interest in my auditioning. That is to say, not until that moment backstage at Grossmont High School when she overheard the other mothers talking about the talent agent and wanted to know more. Her face lit up and it was as though I could see the wheels mentally turning, with thought bubbles practically forming: "My Mario can read and memorize; he's in the advanced class at school. Maybe he could do this commercial stuff?"

Obviously, the fact that I'd been reading since the age of three had been helpful for me in school. No, none of it was literature, certainly no Shakespeare, but my teachers had encouraged me to read aloud in front of the class whenever the opportunity arose. Over time, I'd learned to read and articulate just about anything you put in front of me—whether or not I could comprehend the big words and concepts. But, frankly, as I'd later realize, you don't need to understand when you read off a teleprompter.

Probably the real reason Mom wanted to investigate the possibility of getting me an agent was because, as anyone in my family could attest, I wasn't afraid of the spotlight. Shy I was not. Mom also knew that I could talk to anyone and everyone, carrying on conversations with adults about all kinds of subjects. More than being just a kid who sought attention—which I loved, of course—I cared more about the approval that came from being really good at something like wrestling. So, in her ongoing quest to find ways to keep me active, she most likely saw this as yet another outlet.

After the recital was over, Mom found the opportunity to approach Christine Guerrero, who, it turned out, had been impressed with my dancing. She invited me to come to her office to read for her. And that's how I was discovered: ten years old, in full-on makeup at a dance competition somewhere outside San Diego.

Even though I'd been invited to what to anyone else could have been my big break, I was in no rush to meet with the agent—frankly, I didn't care one way or the other. Knowing next to nothing about show business, I didn't necessarily want to be an actor or performer on TV. Who even knew what being on TV meant or what it would be like?

My mother didn't push it. She asked me, "*Mijo*, do you want to talk to this lady and do a scene? You can see if you like it and if she likes you, and it might be something you can do?"

If my mom asked, I was going to do it. See what I mean? That's the kind of son I was.

At the meeting, Christine Guerrero began by matter-of-factly talking about the ins and outs of the business. Then she smiled and asked, "Mario, would you read something for me?"

That didn't sound too terrible. I agreed and she handed me a dirty, wrinkled piece of paper with commercial copy on it. No doubt she had used this same script for countless auditions. The commercial was for an insurance company and the copy told a sad story about a boy who lost his dog in the rain. Reading it, I knew to lift my eyes from the page and, as I did, I saw the agent staring at me intently.

When I was done reading, she made a note and then looked up, turning first to my mother and then to me, saying that she would very much like to work with us.

All these years later as I think back to how this played out, from the moment in the wings before the dance recital at the high school to this meeting with my first talent agent, I still think it's ironic that I broke into show business at the age of ten because of dancing.

My dad thinks it's ironic, as he says, that I've never had a real job. Because I started acting so young, I've basically always been a professional, except for one part of a summer when I worked for one of Dad's landscaping businesses. Well, that was short-lived employment and he did it mostly to help me during a lag in my performing career. So I guess he's right. I've never had a real job. But as far as *non*-real jobs go, I've been working since I was in the fifth grade, in multiple arenas of the entertainment industry. Bottom line? Working as a child served one very important purpose: it kept me out of *some* trouble.

After I signed with my new San Diego–based agent, she immediately began submitting me for local ads and I went right to work doing print. It happened fast and I didn't have time to think too much about the process. I'd just show up and they'd take pictures of me. Next thing you knew, I'd see the pictures in a little cat-alog.

The first gig was a catalog ad for a bank. The graphics read, *"Sonríe"*—smile—"you're in bank country." With a baseball theme, I was dressed in a catcher's uniform and wore a catcher's mask on top of my head, while I had my arm around this little white kid, who was the pitcher. We were both smiling.

As the print jobs added up, Mom collected copies but never put my pictures on the fridge or on the wall, or anywhere in the house. She kept albums, but unlike awards from competitions or commendations from school, she didn't put anything on display—maybe so as not to make Marissa feel left out. My sister probably wouldn't have minded, though, with all that she had going for her. Very smart, funny, and really pretty, my sister excelled at every-thing. Besides being a dancer too, she was a star student, went on to be captain of her cheerleading squad in high school, and later would go on to graduate college on the dean's list. The joke re-mained that even though I was the older brother, I had to keep up.

For his part, Dad was supportive of this new activity, just as with everything else I did—which now also included karate. He took me to auditions sometimes too, depending on his and Mom's work schedules. He didn't discourage what I was doing, but nei-ther he nor Mom made a big deal out of it. Their attitude was that as long as I was enjoying the modeling and acting thing, they ap-proved. The upshot was that I was allowed to have a normal, well-rounded childhood. If I wasn't wrestling, I'd be happy dancing. If I wasn't dancing, I'd be happy doing karate. If it wasn't that, I'd be happy doing a little play. I never wanted to be a star. But here I was, within a short amount of time, a child working in the business.

Before long, my agent had built a name for the agency and began to get commercial calls from casting directors outside San

Diego. Then the calls started coming in from Los Angeles casting offices, which meant better and bigger bookings, with the potential to book a higher caliber of commercial—regional or even national—that could pay well and elevate exposure. But the drive from Chula Vista to Hollywood was two hours or more in traffic. That was four-plus hours round-trip after school that Mom or Dad would have to arrange to drive me, juggling their own work schedules.

They could have decided against making the trek. Instead, Mom figured, "Why not?" Dad thought it was worth a shot.

Thankfully, they cast blindly back then. Unlike later commercial casting sheets that specify ethnicity—African-American, Asian, Hispanic, white, and so on—the calls back then were often for children and youth of a specific age range. Agents would submit headshots or photo composites of their top talent in those categories and the casting people would go through hundreds if not thousands of submissions, pick out the kids who looked like they could possibly fit the bill, and then notify the agent of an appointment for the young client. Most calls were initially for every type under the sun—cute kids, offbeat kids, charmers, wisecrackers, annoying show-offs, and even shyer kids who just happened to maybe have a memorable look that the camera liked. Most of the time, as we waited outside to be seen by a casting director, there would be copy to read and rehearse, or a storyboard to study so you would know the setup when your name was called.

Sometimes we were asked to read or memorize a few lines or improvise, based on the scenario given. Very quickly, I got the hang of the process—how to slate for the camera and give my name, how to listen as well as respond on cue. After a few trips up the 405 freeway and back, I began to get callbacks before landing my first commercial, and then another one after that. Now, in a very short amount of time, I had made it onto TV. What usually happens next for kid actors in Hollywood is that after getting booked on commercials, you start being sent out on theatrical auditions for roles in movies and on television series. Or at least that's what happened for me. One of my first theatrical calls was for *A.K.A. Pablo*, a new ABC sitcom that was created by none other than Norman Lear—an incredible opportunity.

Producer Norman Lear—a TV legend if ever there was one—was responsible for such groundbreaking shows as *All in the Family*, *The Jeffersons*, *Maude*, and *Sanford and Son*. *A.K.A. Pablo*, starring the stand-up comedian Paul Rodriguez, was to be the first show in the history of U.S. television to feature an all-Latino cast. When I arrived at the audition to read for the role of young Tomas Del Gato on the series, I realized at once why an audition like this was described as a cattle call. There were hordes of actors being seen for the different parts and we were being herded in and out of the casting director's office like cattle. Because I didn't realize the importance of the opportunity at the time, I didn't know to get nervous. When my name was finally called, I went in, slated for the camera, did the reading, and after almost no time emerged from the room and went to find my mother so we could drive back to San Diego.

Casting directors would often say, "Very nice" or "Thank you, Mario; that was great," which translated as "Don't call us; we'll call you." So I learned early on not to expect a callback to come in—until it did. But for a big prime-time show, it's not just one callback. It's like March Madness, where you go from cattle call to a callback with the casting director and the rest of the casting associates for the network and then to a second callback with the director, to a third callback with all the producers and writers in the room. If you make it that far, you get to go to the big semifinal round where you meet executive producers. And last but not least, when you have gone the distance, you go in front of the network. The suits. You don't know their names or their exact positions, but they have the ultimate say-so. Going to network is where many an actor's career has been made or gone up in flames.

So at long last, after six round-trips from Chula Vista to Hollywood, I went to the network and the word came back that I was cast as a regular on *A.K.A. Pablo*. From the very first table reading, where I got a chance to get to know Paul Rodriguez and the rest of the cast and crew, I felt like this TV family wasn't so different from mine. The story line was based on Paul's real-life journey as a stand-up comic and incorporated his use of humorous stereotypes about his own Mexican background—but that didn't always go over well with his TV family. Everything was exaggerated: a huge Mexican family, all twenty-five of us, living in one house, complete with noisy chickens in the family room and piñatas in the front yard. I mean, every bad, insulting Mexican stereotype. The one that stands out for me was a scene that featured Paul Rodriguez doing a comedy bit where he would say, "People ask me for my American Express card . . . this is my Mexican Express card," and then he'd produce a Rambo-type knife.

Here's another classic line, for example, that Paul might say jokingly, only to offend his family members: "Latinos are black, white, brown, beige. What does that say about our ancestors? We'll sleep with anybody!"

Norman Lear, a genius known for pushing both the cultural and political edges, understood that *A.K.A. Pablo* was important for advancing the representation of Latinos on television and in media in general. Even at ten years old, I knew that there were very few Hispanic actors on television back then and even fewer Mexicans, unless you want to include some of the Clint Eastwood movies that came on TV now and then. In the early days of comedy, we had Cuban-born Desi Arnaz, who with Lucille Ball and their *I Love Lucy* pioneered the genre of sitcoms. Then there was Puerto Rican Freddie Prinze, a brilliant comedian and actor, in the seventies. And then, in the eighties, *A.K.A. Pablo* showed up as the first Mexican-American show ever and helped put Paul on the map, as well as featuring such gifted actors as Hector Elizondo and Joe Santos. As Tomas, I played one of Paul's nephews. Working on the show was like being part of one big family party—the perfect foray for me into the world of TV acting.

On one of the episodes, I was told that Bea Arthur would be guest starring and I was going to do my scenes with her. Of course, I knew who she was and what an amazing comedic actress she was. But then meeting her in person, I found that her warmth and humor filled the room. When we started to rehearse, I had a hard time keeping a straight face, even though I was one of those kids who could also be serious. She was just masterful with timing and delivery. Besides being an exceptionally talented woman, she was so nice to me on set. When I'd ask her questions and get her feedback on my delivery, she was helpful and sweet, and then she'd invite me to join her for lunch so we could continue the conversation.

During the shooting of the thirteen episodes ordered by ABC, I continued to go to regular public school at home in Chula Vista. Industry insiders have always been shocked to hear that. Actually, I'm one of very few kids who grew up in the business and remained in public school all the way to graduation. When I was needed on the set on days when I was supposed to be at school, I'd go to school on the set. My feeling is that the attention I was given ultimately led to a better education. We went for a minimum of three or four hours straight, and then we'd call bank hours for later on. The advantage was being able to study one-on-one with personal tutors on all the subjects, as opposed to being in a class with forty kids where you don't have to really pay attention. On the set, there were no recesses, no playtime. The message was implicit but clear: you were there to go to school and you focused. Then, of course, when that episode's filming was over, I just went back to school, to my friends and classmates and all the regular activities that were part of staying active and too busy for trouble.

When I got *A.K.A. Pablo*, which premiered in March 1984, my contract from the network and production company didn't cover lodging or any of my expenses. I was making maybe twelve hundred dollars per episode. That seems like a lot of money, and it is, but after deducting agent commissions and taxes, plus the expense of lodging and gas and food, you might only have half left.

But leave it to my budget-savvy parents to keep expenses down. For instance, after doing research, Dad located a couple of forty-dollar-a-night motels on the Sunset Strip.

"Sunset Strip?" Sounded cool to me. Other than the various casting offices around town and the studio where *A.K.A. Pablo* was shot, I hadn't seen much of Hollywood at all.

When we drove down the Strip and pulled up to the first motel where we planned on staying, my head was on a swivel as I took it all in—the bright flashing neon signs of bars and clubs, the tricked-out lowriders cruising the boulevard, the spiraling spotlight from Grauman's Chinese Theatre not too far away, the mix of tourists and seedy-looking characters that were all part of the nightlife.

After we checked in to our room, my dad went to take a shower and I, eager to investigate, snuck out to play in the parking lot with some kids whose families were staying at the same motel. The parking lot was open to the bright lights of the Strip and I couldn't help overhearing an argument between what turned out to be a pimp and the first hooker I'd ever seen in real life. They looked straight out of 1970s central casting, like a pair you'd see on an episode of *Starsky & Hutch*. Or the movie *Shaft*. He was big, barrel-chested, and dressed in a long dark coat while she was a platinum blonde in high platform pumps and a tight little low-cut dress that did grab my attention. The pimp starting yelling about money or something and then began to smack her around until she started to yell back at him. With that, he shoved her really hard, she fell to the ground, and her dress went backward and up, revealing that she didn't have any underwear on.

Whoa! I must have gasped out loud. That was the first time I'd seen a woman basically naked—and it was definitely an eye-opening experience. Chula Vista was the barrio, for sure, but I'd never seen anything like that back home.

Suffice it to say, I had a lot more to learn about the perils of street life and sex and women and all that went with them. Still, I couldn't wait to get home to tell my cousins about the sights on Sunset Strip.

As fast as good fortune can arrive in show business, it can be gone just as fast, and sometimes even faster. So it was with *A.K.A. Pablo*. Norman Lear was a visionary who knew that a TV show about a Mexican family was an idea whose time had come. But it seemed that in 1984 he was ahead of his time, or so the network decided. Though we shot thirteen episodes, we were canceled after the sixth episode aired, so the remaining seven episodes never aired. At the time, critics were for the most part brutal. Here's a fun fact: in 2002, *TV Guide* ranked the series number forty-five on its "50 Worst TV Shows of All Time." That's harsh, considering that many top-rated syndicated sitcoms didn't gather followings until their second seasons; networks must invest in the time to let that happen.

That said, I was lucky to learn early in the game how to accept the ups and downs and then move on. And in addition to getting a crash course in the basics of being a child actor on a series, I honed some real skills in comedy acting and auditioning. As it happened, whenever the script called for one of the kids to handle extensive dialogue, we would have to audition against each other to be given that scene—even though we were already on the show. On the episode called "I Don't Want to Be a Mexican," the writers had written the lines for one of the kids and I really wanted to prove I could handle the acting the role required. After trying out most of the younger actors in the cast, they gave it to me. Winning those additional lines wasn't a big deal, but it made me so happy! That's apparently how I was wired as a kid: to win at anything made me happy.

And yet, in the months that followed the cancellation of *A.K.A. Pablo*, I had a taste of not winning—another reality check that, in hindsight, I can appreciate. Most of the calls I went on in LA at this point were again for commercials. I didn't go on a ton of auditions, though, because in this period the sponsors were starting to be more specific about the type and look they wanted and somehow I fell through the cracks. Either I wasn't "ethnic" enough or I wasn't all-American enough. And I didn't get a lot of jobs that I auditioned for—more than I could count.

"Mario, have you considered changing your name? Perhaps to something less ethnic" was a suggestion I started hearing during this time. Agents and manager types wanted me to make the change to widen my appeal.

My dad wouldn't even consider it. He said, "Mario Lopez is your name. That's what I named you. You should be proud of it."

Arguments for a name change continued from others. After all, they argued, the respected Mexican actor Anthony Quinn had changed his name from Antonio Rodolfo Quinn Oaxaca. I had a friend, Miguel Gil De Montes, who changed his name to Mark Roberts. The list went on and on. But Dad was right: Mario Lopez was my name. And as entertaining as it was to think about cool wrestling names I could take on, I got through the name-changing phase and went back to auditioning for commercials.

After I was fortunate enough to book a McDonald's commercial, I went in on a milk spot that was about this kid who throws a basketball in a hoop, but over his shoulder without looking behind him. And the line to a cow watching was, "Hey, Mr. Moo. What do you say?" Instead of amping it up, I said it really cool, as if I were trying to con Mr. Moo. The casting director laughed out loud because that laid-back delivery wasn't what she was expecting. She read the cow's line, "Fresh moo juice makes my day."

At first I wasn't sure her laughing was a good thing. I'd gone into that audition wearing a leather jacket, like Fonzie, and thought I was being super cool by trying to imitate a much older guy, as opposed to how I thought a little kid would read that line.

Sometimes it pays to follow your creative instincts and do something different, as long as it's not too over-the-top. I ended up getting the job. That was a big national commercial and I can still remember it. A young actor could make a lot of money doing commercials back in those days, and for a kid those earnings could be put into a savings account and help pay for college. And earning money like that can be very meaningful—especially for a ten-year-old kid whose parents were from blue-collar backgrounds and who'd never had the means to go to college.

Still, my mom and dad didn't emphasize the money. As long as I liked performing and as long as I wasn't booking jobs just to feel proud of myself—a common issue for child actors—my parents continued to support me all the way. When I think back to that

two-hour schlep up the 405 to Hollywood and then back—
sometimes for an audition that lasted all of thirty seconds—I'm
stunned. My parents were champs, never questioning whether it
was worth it, even when I'd get two or three auditions in a week.
Because I was mostly being sent out for calls seeking a Mexican
boy, these auditions tended not to be on the same day as they could
be for commercial actors going out on all kinds of calls.

To my parents' credit, they also refrained from treating me
any differently once I began to work regularly. Nor was I allowed to
develop an inflated sense of self from earning some good money,
when that came, along with the added attention. Our family's lifestyle didn't change, and just because I was making my own money
didn't mean I lived in Neverland. If I got excellent grades, I might
be given the new edition video game system or some of the latest
kicks, but not much more than that. My upbringing would not have
let me become Famous Mario or some showbiz child tyrant. Even
as a working kid actor, I still had chores at home and a mandate for
school to come first. My parents did not indulge behavior that
could be seen as me getting all "Hollywoody." The message from
my parents, no matter how famous I later became, was that I was
still one of their two Lopez kids, part of a huge loving extended
family from Chula Vista, California. Period.

Over the years, I had a chance to meet child actors who became household names and to observe not only the pitfalls but also
how to avoid them. When I met Gary Coleman from *Diff'rent
Strokes*, I didn't warm up to him, mainly because he seemed
spoiled. That does happen when a child professional has a team of
handlers who cater to the young star's every whim while con-
trolling him at the same time. When I worked with the boys in
Menudo—the globally famous Latin boy band that was the One
Direction of its time—I saw how fast you could blow up to become

young superstars of the moment but then how only a few teen idols, like Ricky Martin, get to shine on after their time in the sun. When I met Ricky Schroder, who is a couple of years older than me and was the child star of the series *Silver Spoons,* he was a good example of how to embrace your success yet remain down-to-earth. Ricky befriended me, gave me a personal tour of the Universal lot, and even let me ride his bike around the lot on my own.

Obviously, there are more extreme examples today of young performers who do not fare well when they fall from grace or when their success is so massive that they lose all sense of boundaries. For some it's blowing all their money and for others it's substance abuse and legal problems, including litigation against their own parents. Some come back from the edge, but when your name is Justin Bieber or Miley Cyrus, it's not like you get to go through periods of acting out without the whole world watching.

Those pitfalls are not easy to avoid. I'm one of the few child actors who never went down those roads, thanks to the boundaries my parents set.

The irony in all this is that it's not normal to be a kid who makes money and is famous or becomes recognized out in public, so you need to have strong guidance in keeping a balance between industry work and a normal upbringing. There were ongoing examples of kids on auditions whose pushy mom or dad hung on the casting director's decision, desperate for their progeny to do the family name proud, as if not getting the job would stop the world from turning. It stressed me out just to watch it. My parents, thankfully, went in the opposite direction. My mom was her usual excited self when I did book something, but, like with Dad, it wasn't going to ruin her day if I didn't. There was never a conversation about me having a "career." That can't be healthy for a ten- or eleven-year-old—or even a sixteen-year-old.

After I had such a lucky break as to get a TV series right off the bat, I was able to go back to auditioning without a big job right away and keep my laissez-faire attitude. Me, the high-energy keep-him-out-of-trouble kid, laissez-faire? Well, with sports, no. In the heat of the action, I was a different kind of animal, given the competitiveness I'm wired with. When it came to acting, though, I mainly wanted to do a good job. That may sound inconsistent, but in the end I knew that's all it was to me: a job. It didn't summon the same passion that wrestling did. Acting wasn't a contest that involved a matchup of skills against skills. Acting strengths can be very subjective, and though I enjoyed the challenge of interpreting the lines, it wasn't do-or-die.

And, luckily, that attitude worked to my advantage. Casting directors seemed to like a kid who played it cool, who wasn't desperate for getting a job.

Little did I realize until somewhat later that my easygoing approach to pursuing acting roles would serve me well when it came to dating. Generally, if you play it cool and nonchalant, you'll do much better at getting the girl . . . just like the role.

This is all to tell you that I didn't experience the emotional roller coaster of working and then not working, nor the super high of getting a part along with the super low of being rejected. When a job ended I wasn't crushed; I thought we were just done with it. As an adult, I know what it feels like to be disappointed about a canceled show. But as a kid, I didn't care; I just rolled with it.

At age eleven, I was back to my regular life in public school— back to wrestling, karate, dance, and theater. My parents were still schlepping me to and from LA for auditions. Then, in the fall of 1984, I went in on a call for a new series called *Kids Incorporated*.

Mom recapped the breakdown from my agent as we jumped

in the car to head to LA. All she knew, she said, was, "It's an ensemble show for a teen dance and rock group."

The audition was a cattle call on steroids. Massive. Kids in the thousands were lined up around the block—all looking like we were plucked out of an eighties rock video, most wearing a lot of acid-washed denim, big hair, and neon colors. Talk about being ahead of its time—this audition was exactly what you'd see in later decades with tryouts for *American Idol*, *So You Think You Can Dance*, *The X Factor*, and other reality shows: thousands of people with a dream of being chosen, all standing outside in a seemingly endless line. Having been there myself, I would always have a special place in my heart for kids who become reality show contenders and have to put their talents on the line to be judged.

The *Kids Incorporated* call was not just for actors but for young performers who could sing, dance, and possibly even play an instrument. My dance abilities were strong, but my training at All That Jazz had been limited to jazz and tap, not ballet. I messed around with break dancing and was starting to put a crew together—complete with taking a piece of cardboard to school so I could refine my head spins—but I was ahead of my time and hip-hop was not the well-respected dance genre that it is today. Compared to some of the kids trying out who had trained in ballet and gymnastics since they were in diapers, I had less training but showed in the audition that I could hold my own. As far as singing goes, I had my dad to thank for my years of mariachi singing at local bars and competing in various singing contests. I also had Dad to thank for getting me into drumming. One of his buddies was a drummer and they would let me bang around sometimes, eventually teaching me some basics. After that, I taught myself the rest and loved playing drums whenever I could. Was I any good? Back then, I wasn't bad. I'm not saying I could do the drum solos like I was the fifth member of Led Zeppelin, but, man, I'd love to play as well today as I could at age eleven.

So, between my singing, dancing, and acting, I made it through the gauntlet into the final round of contenders. It's quite possible that playing the drums was the extra factor that helped me land the gig.

Wow, I thought, this was going to be so much fun. And it was. But it was also probably the toughest job I ever had in show business. As soon as I was cast, we went to work right away and were doing three shows per week in Hollywood, at Sunset Gower Studios. We had to practice and perform three concert numbers and multiple dance numbers for each episode. In almost every show, I sang, danced, and played the drums. Like show business boot camp, the production schedule for *Kids* was grueling.

The New York choreographer Duraine Gusman was a tough taskmaster—especially and noticeably with me. We had to learn and master her choreography for five to seven dance numbers a week, a daunting undertaking for the most experienced dancers. Besides the fact that I was one of the less rigorously trained dancers in the ensemble, I was also the youngest member in the cast, so I got my butt kicked. In my own defense, I happened to be a quick study, and when the time came to perform on camera, I was right on the money, killin' it.

But Duraine Gusman was not the epitome of patience. I have a vivid memory of an afternoon in one of the rehearsal halls at Sunset Gower when I was struggling with a couple of eight-counts of complicated choreography. Gusman kept stopping us and shouting at me, saying, "Mario, try it again—you don't have it!" It was embarrassing. When she stopped us a third time and came over to me, shaking her head and saying, "No. Can you not get it? What are you, brain-dead?" or words to that effect, I was shaken.

My dad was in the rehearsal room that day and he was so upset that he stood up and walked out. He told my mom what had happened, saying, "If Gusman had been a man, I would have put him in his place about treating a kid like that, but she's a woman so I held my tongue."

When my mom came to me, ready to read the riot act to our choreographer, I said, "No, don't say anything. It'll make the situation worse."

Sometimes, as my parents saw, you have to let kids fight their own battles. From then on, I doubled down, working even harder, and proved to our choreographer that I could keep up.

Stumbling over some choreography didn't detract from the fun I had every day for the three seasons I was on *Kids*. We were given a feel for what was hot in pop culture, performing hit songs of the day, like "Careless Whisper" by George Michael and "The Warrior" by Patti Smith. And just as on *A.K.A. Pablo*, I worked my way into unplanned acting opportunities as they came up. Since I was primarily in the performing ensemble—not unlike Jennifer Lopez (no relation), who was one of the Fly Girl dancers on the sketch comedy show *In Living Color*—I didn't have many lines. But when the script called for one of us to rap, I vied for the job and got it. How awesome was that? I performed New Edition's "Cool It Now" like it was my own personal theme song. The rap was a reminder that when you've "got a girl who takes her time" you have to take it slow, to "cool it down." That was a breakthrough for me on the show. There is a clip of this, by the way, on YouTube if you want to see that moment in action. Not bad for early vintage rapping. From then on, they started giving me more lines.

Oh, and then, toward the end of 1985, when I was still eleven, I started noticing girls for real—including some of my talented castmates, like the lovely and multitalented Jennifer Love Hewitt, who is still a friend, and also one other vivacious, beautiful fellow eleven-year-old, Stacy, who seemed to think I was sort of cool.

Stacy's parents and mine became friendly and learned from one another that the two of us had crushes on each other. There was something about her that was sort of magical, as if she knew this was the beginning of a career in music. We gravitated toward each other in what I figured was basic flirting. And, sure enough, one day Stacy and I were on a break from shooting, standing back behind the set just talking, and, in the most natural and mutual way possible, both leaned in for a kiss. After that, we stole little kisses whenever possible. There was a lot of kissing, as I recall, but nothing more than that really—all very innocent eleven-year-old affection.

These days whenever I see Stacy—who was Stacy Ferguson back then but now is better known as Fergie, a solo artist after attaining fame and fortune with the Black Eyed Peas—we laugh about the preteen romance we had on *Kids Incorporated*. For me, there's something special about having had my first kiss with Fergie, back before she was a rock star but still on her way to somewhere great.

Although *Kids Incorporated* remains the toughest job I ever worked—as a kid or an adult—it tested my mettle and made me stronger and more resilient as a performer. Those three seasons were long, even if I was doing it part-time. And being pushed by a tough-as-nails choreographer was a challenge that benefited me in the long run. When I left the show, I was a far more well-rounded performer and immensely grateful for the ride.

*Kids* was key in turning me into a youthful Renaissance man, in showbiz terms, because I now had trained to do everything. Between the two series I had been fortunate to develop my chops in multiple disciplines. Most kids who come of age in the entertainment industry are known for doing one thing or another, not for being the classic triple threats you see on Broadway or that used to populate Hollywood in the olden days. There are obviously exceptions—like the phenomenal Justin Timberlake and the gifted Bruno Mars, two dudes who started young and can do it all. But for the most part, nowadays being an all-around young showman is pretty rare.

Of course, being a multifaceted performer would not have been possible without my mother having the foresight to put me in so many damn activities. At a certain point, these different calling cards would make me highly sought after as a young performer. But my life as a professional continued to be balanced with having a normal life as a teenager in between gigs. I wasn't chasing *it*; rather I would let *it* come to me. I never asked for more auditions. Instead, I just responded to the calls, giving my best at the time. Meanwhile, I did theater at school, as in the past, but didn't add more private coaching for voice or acting. Performing was one of the things I did—it wasn't the be-all and end-all to my existence. Part of not becoming all Hollywoody, I believe, was appreciating the steps along the way without needing them to be taking me anywhere other than where I was.

That being the case, after *A.K.A. Pablo* and *Kids Incorporated*, I did an eclectic mix of guest spots on various shows, a few pilots, and continued to do commercials—when I could get them. My favorite guest spot was on the hit sitcom *The Golden Girls*, where I played a Cuban immigrant boy who was going to be deported. This was before the real-life Elián Gonzáles story, but it was similar. On that episode, I was reunited with the one and only Bea Arthur, who again helped me raise my comedic game. Once again, she took me under her wing and made sure I got to know all the Golden Girls. All those women on that show were some of the funniest and gifted women on television.

After that episode and the other guest spots that came along, I kept on doing my thing, which at the time was negotiating my way through junior high and those wild and crazy days of adolescence. High school was just around the corner and so too was my audition for the role of a young lifetime.

# CHAPTER 3

## *SAVED BY THE BELL*

The year was 1989—the end of a decade of excesses that saw the debut of the TV show *The Lifestyles of the Rich and Famous*, an explosion in conspicuous consumption that turned household budget watchers into carefree shopaholics, and a pop culture fiesta that began early on with Madonna's "Material Girl" video that was both fashion manual and theme song for status seeking and accumulating megawealth. For kids growing up eighties-style, that meant wearing the top brands, with designer labels and logos sewn on the outside of clothes. It meant owning the latest video games and the newest sneakers that cost more than dress shoes, and everyone climbing in Mom's minivan to be driven to the growing list of after-school activities that we all were increasingly expected to enjoy.

This was the decade when cable, combined with VCRs, revolutionized the way America and the world consumed media. By 1989 TV watching was gauged at an average of seven hours a day for most households, and it was also a time when we finally started seeing more stars from diverse backgrounds. The eighties were the years when nerds first began to make lots of money—with computer brainiacs like Steve Wozniak, Steve Jobs, and Bill Gates all starting their journeys as masters of the universe. As proven by the 1984 movie *Revenge of the Nerds*, you could apparently be a geek and still be cool.

As we prepared for big cultural changes coming up in the 1990s, over at NBC's Entertainment Division the late Brandon Tartikoff was in search of a new series to help bolster the network's Saturday morning lineup. A visionary, Tartikoff had been instrumental in turning NBC around—from last place among the major networks in the early 1980s to eventually being the top-rated network, a position it held for five consecutive seasons. Shows that proved Brandon Tartikoff famously had the Midas touch included *Hill Street Blues, L.A. Law, Cheers, Family Ties, The Cosby Show, Knight Rider,* and *Seinfeld.* For *Miami Vice,* as legend has it, he saw a perfect niche to fill and pitched the network his high-concept premise with two words: "MTV cops."

Instead of coming up with a brand-new idea that would appeal to a captive Saturday morning audience of younger viewers, Tartikoff decided to develop a spin-off of an existing show called *Good Morning, Miss Bliss,* about a wonderful teacher and her students. Originally developed as a pilot by NBC, the series was rejected by the network and then picked up by the Disney Channel, which ordered thirteen episodes to air in 1988. Due to poor ratings, Disney decided to drop the show before the first season was over. At that point, NBC reclaimed the series and—between Tartikoff and Peter Engel, the show's creator and producer—it was decided to retool the story line from being about the teacher into focusing more on the high school students and their lives. At first, Engel wanted to call the spin-off *When the Bell Rings,* but Tartikoff suggested *Saved by the Bell.* And we know how that turned out.

For those who had followed the story line of *Good Morning,* there were some changes in store. The new series no longer featured the beloved Miss Bliss (played by the classy Hayley Mills, a former child star of Disney movie fame), and the setting had moved from a school in Indianapolis to the fictional Bayside High School in the Palisades, here in Los Angeles. For *Saved by the Bell* (*SBTB*), the producers dropped some of the characters but kept three of them: the show's lead, Zack Morris (Mark-Paul Gosselaar), the popular, charming kid who always gets himself in trouble with his questionable schemes that never work out; the über-nerdy Screech Powers (Dustin Diamond); and the high-energy gossip and fashionista Lisa Turtle (Lark Voorhies). Three new characters were added: the all-American cheerleader and girl-next-door Kelly Kapowski (a role that would go to Tiffani Thiessen); the smart, strong-willed crusader for causes like women's lib and the environment, Jessie Spano (to be played by Elizabeth Berkley); and the transfer student, A. C. Slater, an army brat whose dad is in the military and has been relocated to the Palisades in Southern California.

When I first heard that I had an appointment to read for the role of A. C. Slater on this new NBC spin-off, to me it was just another audition. I had no concept of the magnitude of the opportunity. In general, auditions for high school–aged talent were few and far between. This was still the eighties, after all, before the heyday of Nickelodeon and smart sitcoms featuring the lives of teenagers like me and my friends. At fifteen years old, with my hormones in charge, frankly, I was more interested in chasing girls than trekking up to LA to read for a part that had barely been sketched out on paper, other than that Slater was the new kid in school.

My work ethic was more powerful than my hormones and I wasn't going to disappoint Mom, so there was never a thought of not doing the audition. But did I care? Not so much. With twenty-twenty hindsight, I clearly didn't have my priorities in check—although what teenager does? At that point, I was crazy for this one girl in Chula Vista, and the time away from her was almost painful! Plus, an audition meant missing practice with my wrestling team—

yet another reason not to care so much about whether or not I'd get the part. Later on, when I was making the transition from child actor to adult actor and TV personality, I lost the carefree attitude and started to care much more, especially after gaining a better understanding of the stakes of each opportunity.

The *SBTB* audition process was a true gauntlet. Thousands of kids, all really different from one another, were up for the part of Slater. When I read for the show's casting director, Robin Lippin, I was my usual cool self, reading the scene almost as if this guy A. C. Slater had my easygoing personality—kind of Rico Suave but with the hint of an edge thrown in for good measure.

Robin gave me the usual "That was really great, Mario. Thank you so much for coming in!" and I hightailed it out of there, forgetting anything about the part until the call arrived that I'd be meeting the NBC casting associates, and then the call after that for the next level of decision makers in the huge hierarchy. All the while, the casting for all three of the new roles was equally intense.

As far as I knew, there were no other Mexican or Latino kids who had auditioned for the part, or at least none were under consideration for it as the numbers were whittled down. The name A. C. Slater certainly didn't have the Hispanic ring to it that many of the roles I went in on had. The good news was that, from what I saw in the process, they cast blindly for *SBTB* and wound up with a fairly diverse cast, especially for the time.

Once I was in the hunt, I started to become invested and soon that competitive part of me kicked in. Every time I made it to the next level, nothing was a given—only that I was alive for yet another round.

When I went to network, finally, I knew the job to play A. C. Slater was down to the two of us left standing: me and one other teen actor who was more of a Dustin Diamond sort of nerd type than a street-smart bad-boy type. One of the producers really liked the other guy. But it appeared the network could be leaning toward me. As in the past, I hoped that my cool attitude was going to tip the scales in my favor. Plus, as an athlete in good shape from years of competitive wrestling, I had the right stature and build to play a traditional jock. There wasn't one yet on the show.

Still, even with those things going for me, when I walked out of the reading for the network, I knew there was a possibility they would test other actors or ask me to come back to read for them again. You just never knew.

"C'mon, *mijo*," Mom said, after the audition. "We have a long ride home."

On what was normally at least a two-hour drive—at times twice that long—we found ourselves in bumper-to-bumper traffic. This was going to be a long ride.

"You hungry?" Mom asked after we stopped to fill up with gas.

Sounded good to me. The traffic had given me a headache and the change of scenery helped break up the trip.

Once we'd settled into our booth in the diner just off the freeway, Mom thought it might be worth it to go to the pay phone and see what the feedback was and find out whether I needed to come back for another audition. Five minutes later, my mother came back with a blank look on her face.

"What's wrong?"

"Nothing." Then she cracked up and gave me the news. My agent told Mom she had just heard from Robin Lippin, the casting director.

"You got the part! You are going to be A. C. Slater on *Saved by the Bell*."

As they say in Hollywood, good news travels fast.

We hugged and high-fived, finished up our meal, and drove the rest of the way home. As cool as we all were, that's when I started to get excited about the prospect of being part of something of this scope. But I could not have fathomed how it was going to change my life in the ways that it would. The money was great, for sure, more than ever before—three thousand dollars an episode was damn good for a fifteen-year-old. It wasn't *Friends* money, by any means. And as before, we had to cover all of our own expenses, including lodging and gas. A prime-time sitcom would have been different. Since it was a Saturday morning show, the series had limited reach and sponsor opportunities. If my agent in that era had been more savvy—or if we'd had any guess about how popular the show was going to be—I would have tried to avoid signing a ridiculous contract that stipulated we couldn't make any money off merchandising or endorsements. The show was the first of its kind and we didn't really know how much pull we had as actors. File this lesson under the heading of "Live and learn."

A.C. wasn't originally slated to be Latino or a wrestler. The producers hadn't planned for him to be a drummer either, or a break dancer. He wasn't supposed to be any of these things that I already had under my belt. His ethnicity may have once been conceived as Italian, like Vinnie on *Welcome Back, Kotter*, but when I was cast, that went out the window. That was when the producers did something I'd never before encountered.

When I went in to shake hands with the powers that be, I was invited into a meeting with the writers and asked about some of my interests. After I started mentioning a few, one of the writers asked, "Would you mind writing down everything you like to do, any special skills, extracurricular activities, or after-school involvement?" This was what they did with all the leads and, as we would discover, it yielded great storytelling results.

Once again, my mother's master plan was paying off. When I finished, I had one hell of a long list, thanks to Mom. Lo and behold, the producers decided to incorporate many of my real-life skills and interests into the fictional character of A. C. Slater. As I found out, before I was their guy, the vision for Slater as a new kid in school was seen as a teenage boy with a lot of street smarts because of having to move a lot as an army brat. Kind of shady. Scrawny. Very mysterious. I imagine they were aiming for a bad boy like Judd Nelson's character from *The Breakfast Club*. But Slater turned into a jock because that's what I was. And that's what they built the story lines around.

When our first episode aired in August 1989, we were shown on prime time that week and the next before moving to our Saturday morning slot. Right away NBC knew that Brandon Tartikoff had another winner on his hands. And they hadn't seen nothin' yet.

The summer schedule for shooting the show became second nature to me, but in the early stages required a learning curve as we went through the script in different ways throughout the week in preparation to film on Fridays. We would do the table read on Monday—where we would actually sit around a table in a room with all the actors, writers, directors, producers, and some other important network execs. We would go through the script, making the dialogue our own as the writers invariably laughed at their own jokes. On cue! As the week progressed, the director would start blocking and rehearsing the scenes as the show began to take form. By the second day we'd be given a new script with various line and structural changes and go on to rehearse that at the end of the day. The day after that, there'd be even more changes and we'd work up to another run-through. Then, on Thursday, we had camera block-ing. On Friday during the daytime, we had more rehearsal and we taped some scenes on a closed set, just to have them in the can or to add in later.

Finally, Friday night was showtime—complete with a live au-dience of more than two hundred people. After we wrapped set, we'd hurry out of there to enjoy the weekend off and on Monday we started it all over again.

The appeal of the show was evident to me early in the process. Shooting in front of a live audience is an adrenaline rush. The en-ergy from fans is so powerful, and at the start I couldn't believe it when I heard they were screaming for me. When producers intro-duced me that very first time, right before we taped our first epi-sode, I had a truly out-of-body experience.

The announcer's voice proclaimed, "And playing Slater . . . Mario Lopez!" as I ran out, hit my mark in front of the set, and greeted the audience.

"Mario!" Girls in the audience shrieked, calling my real name, and "Slater!" all while screaming and waving their arms. The au-dience was full of girls, lots of girls, including girls who knew me from other shows and girls who had never seen me before. Wow! As Slater, the new kid, I definitely was given a full-on welcome.

Of course, it was really Zack's show. Each episode was seen through his character's perspective, with dialogue that he would deliver straight to the camera—like Ferris Bueller in a comedy con-text or, in drama, like Ray Liotta in *Goodfellas* (a favorite of mine), where the protagonist breaks the fourth wall and talks directly to the audience. That aspect of the show really lent a quirky, ahead-of-the-curve feeling to a Saturday morning time slot, setting trends in TV that still sometimes seem fresh today.

Meanwhile, our costume, hair, and makeup departments saw

to it that we all looked like trendy teenagers, adorning us in the fashion style of the late 1980s and early 1990s as we moved into a new decade. When I first sat down with the team in hair and makeup, they showed me their ideas for A. C. Slater.

Hairstyles—or wigs, as I refer to them—can define a character's image or ruin it. The wig is a key element that has always been important to me as a performer. My motto that I love to quote before stepping foot on set for the camera: "If the wig's tight, the show's tight." So, when the hair and makeup people showed me their drawings for Slater's hair, I loved the action-adventure tough-guy look they were going for. Kind of like Steven Seagal of that era (without the little ponytail) or Mel Gibson in the *Lethal Weapon* movies.

"Let's do it," I agreed, thinking the wig would be tight.

Only later did I figure out that unintentionally my wig for *SBTB* was a Jheri curl mullet. I didn't even know I had a mullet. It was just the style of the era, like Seagal and Gibson, and I liked looking like them, but getting my hair to obey the laws of mullet-dom was a major undertaking.

First of all, unlike both of my parents, who have curly hair, mine is naturally straight. My mom—whose hair is super curly, almost kinky—looked at me one day when I was beginning my acting career, pointed to a chair in the kitchen, and said, "Come here, *mijo.*"

Up until that time period, my hair had been kind of wavy. Not exactly curly like hers, but not what you'd call straight. But over time the waves slowly vanished and my hair straightened out on its own.

So that day Mom, who must have been some kind of closet stylist, decided to try out an "at home" perm on me. The smell was horrible and it burned my scalp, but I blindly trusted her to know what she was doing. In fact, the classic curl worked on me—so much so that later on, when she stopped the perms, casting people would ask if I could curl it again so that, in their words, I could be "more ethnic," which tended to mean more Puerto Rican.

Having had to curl it so many times during my career as a child actor, I had no problem with getting regular salon perms for *Saved by the Bell*—although once I left the show, that was it for me and curling my hair. For good.

To keep my already permed and mullet-cut wig tight for *SBTB*, I had to get into hair and makeup before anyone else in the cast could—just so they didn't die of asphyxiation. Once the hairdresser finished the styling, our mission was to keep it that way. In theory, this should not have been so daunting. All the classic entertainers—Dean Martin, Sammy Davis Jr., Frank Sinatra—used tons of hair product. But I doubt they came close to what my damn hair required. Besides a cauldron of hairspray, I supplemented with every product on the shelf: gels, more sprays, mousse, anything I could find. I even tried old-school products like Brylcreem and something called Tres Flores.

"What the . . . ?" began one of the hairdressers on the show when she saw me open it up and smelled the petroleum aroma reeking out of it.

"Tres Flores," I explained. "It's what all the cholos wear—even my dad used to use it on his hair to keep it in place." Then I fessed up, admitting that Tres Flores is, basically, Mexican Vaseline.

I'm glad I didn't walk near any open flames or I would have caught on fire. The only real problem was that my hair would get a little too sticky and wet from all the product and would drip, leaving stains on the back of my silk-collared shirts.

Other than all that, the wig was tight. Before long, salons for boys and men were being deluged with requests for the A. C. Slater look.

My wardrobe on the show—never chosen by me—was also intended to reflect trends that high school kids would care about. For Slater, that translated to Z. Cavaricci parachute pants. I've never worn so many pleated baggy jeans with double buckles in my life. I was the king of Z. Cavariccis and rayon shirts, as well as neon tank tops. Everyone had their own signature look that fit the times and their character. As preppy Zack, Mark-Paul wore a lot of sweaters with some crazy eighties patterns on them, like Ferris Bueller, and he was always pushing up the sleeves. Tiffani, as Kelly, was dressed classically as the sporty, all-American cheer-leader. As Lisa, our resident fashion know-it-all, Lark became the hat maven, while Elizabeth, as the intellectual Jessie, was the queen of vests. Let's not even get started on Dustin as Screech. Between his mismatched colors and patterns and his suspenders, he was a poster boy for fashion misses—*Revenge of the Nerds* all the way.

These details helped to make *SBTB* a different kind of high school show. In that time period, it was almost unheard of for actual teenagers to play teenagers on television. In contrast, the hit series *Beverly Hills, 90210* used twentysomethings to play teenagers. *SBTB*'s realness resonated with our fans.

Another trend that worked to our benefit was that when we went on the air, Hollywood was enjoying the heyday of the new Brat Pack—Rob Lowe, Emilio Estevez, Andrew McCarthy, Tom Cruise, and Matt Dillon. We all looked up to those cool young guns, practically worshipping this group of actors, then in their twenties, as they came into their prime. As a new generation of young entertainers, we were positioned to follow in their footsteps and thought of as being on the rise—fresh blood with lots of potential. And like the Brat Pack gang, our group of *SBTB* leads was pretty tight.

We came from different backgrounds, not surprisingly given our diverse casting. Yet I was the only one of the cast members who went to an actual high school that had thousands of students; my castmates either were homeschooled or went to private schools with very small classes. The other kids in the cast weren't all from rich families necessarily, but I was probably from a much lower income bracket than any of my fellow *SBTB* crew. None of that mattered, though. We all got along off-screen as much as we did on-screen.

Let me amend that. Not everyone got along with Screech aka Dustin Diamond. I did, but maybe I was the exception. He was one of those dorky kids who thought it was hilarious to take Polaroids of his genitals and leave the photos all over the set. Annoying as that was, it was in keeping with his TV persona.

Mark-Paul, on the other hand, was a lot shyer than his more outgoing alter ego, Zack. Behind the scenes, he was nothing like the hot-to-trot Zack and really not yet into the dating, social scene that interested me. After our intensive schedule, on weekends I was gung ho, ready to go out, party, and have some fun.

After most Friday night tapings, I'd ask Mark-Paul, "Hey, man, wanna hang out?" and invite him to an after-show party with friends of mine and some of the girls in the cast and their friends.

"Thanks, but . . . that's not my thing," he'd answer diplomatically, and then mention that his mom wouldn't let him. Very protective, she never really let him hang out. He was sheltered that way, though he was a great guy with a lot of talent, and the social thing wasn't a big deal for him.

Needless to say, I was still Mario Lopez from Chula Vista, who had grown up with *"Mi casa es su casa"* and "The more the merrier." I was still the same high-energy kid who was used to hanging out with cousins and friends, now enjoying the camaraderie of going out and getting together with my *SBTB* buddies—still instigating whatever fun and action I could. When I was fifteen going on sixteen, girls were high on that list.

Whether romance flared or not, each of the three female leads on the show was like family to me. Interestingly enough, the role of Lisa Turtle in *Good Morning, Miss Bliss* was not originally written as African-American, but Lark's reading for the producers was apparently so good they rewrote the character to fit her background. In the years after *SBTB*, Lark went on to do soaps and the two of us would both later land on *The Bold and the Beautiful*, though not at the same time. Still, whenever we see each other, we have that connection from our days at Bayside High.

Originally, the role of Lisa Turtle was written as half Jewish, but that changed when Lark got the role. In another twist, Jessie's role wasn't written as Jewish, even though the producers cast the beautiful, tall, lanky, and Jewish Elizabeth Berkley in the role. Elizabeth and I were buddies from the word go. To this day I'm probably closer to her than anyone else from the cast. Besides being very sexy—as evidenced by her later performance in the movie *Showgirls*, in which she bared all—Elizabeth is smart, quick, and funny. And we make each other laugh. When I watch reruns of our scenes and running bits where Jessie calls me a chauvinist "pig" and I just flirt with her and call her "Mama," I can tell how much we inhabited those characters. Even though our Jessie and Slater were hot and heavy for most of the show, we never had a make-out scene, which probably made our friendship easier. Elizabeth and I had a very brother/sister type relationship. And still do.

Although my heart beat for Elizabeth on-screen, I can tell you now that off-screen I set my sights on Tiffani Thiessen. Now remember—I'm the cool guy and know better than to show my interest right away. Except that I was pretty sure at that first table read when I looked across the room and saw this gorgeous girl glancing up at me under lowered eyelashes that she was almost blushing. Unless I was really mistaken, the attraction was mutual and instantaneous.

A slow burn of a flirtation began, but not much happened. Then, after shooting a few episodes, Tiffani mentioned that she did have a boyfriend. A much older boyfriend. So that was the end of that.

Or so I thought until sometime later, a few years into the show's run, when she mentioned that she and the guy had broken up. Interesting. Not rushing into anything, we just started spending more time together off set. What was dating a costar of a teen series like? We did what teenagers do on dates. We went to movies, went out to eat, hung out at parties, danced together. She was a sweetheart who reminded me of a young Priscilla Presley, and I'll admit to feeling as cool as Elvis with her on my arm. When the romance later became official, I got a kick out of the fact that she agreed to wear my real-life letterman jacket—awarded for four years of high school wrestling.

As a high school guy who was known to date around a lot, I thought that being loyal to Tiffani was the right thing to do. But I can't say that I was capable at that age of following through on my noble intentions. There was so much beauty everywhere and I had so much affection to share. That said, my relationship with Tiffani was off and on, but when we were on I did at least try to limit my free agency, shall we say.

Now that I think about it, I'm grateful that Facebook, Twitter, and *TMZ* weren't around when I was a teen and a twentysomething. Most likely I would not have gotten away with the crazier

escapades that played themselves out at different stages and probably would have wound up with a lot more drama and heartache. As
it was, though, I had the best of all worlds. Once again, even with
lessons still to learn, I lucked out.

O ne of the happiest days of these years had nothing to do with
the popularity surrounding *SBTB* or with rites of passage of
dating girls or at high school. The day I almost cried for joy came
when Mom announced to me and Marissa, "Kids, starting on Monday, I am going to be a full-time mother."

My sister and I, talking at the same time, asked what had happened.

Mom went on to say that Dad had found a new position—a
real job with benefits that would provide the family the security
and financial support that would finally make it possible for her to
quit her job at the phone company.

After we finished hugging and high-fiving, my mom pointed
out that it was going to be much easier now to get me back and forth
to Hollywood without my having to miss out on all the important
parts of going to high school in Chula—to wrestling matches,
prom, homecoming, and all the rest of normal life for high school
kids.

And I'm so grateful that my mom was able and willing to help
me do that. As my luck would have it, we shot most of our season in
the summertime so that during the school year we could maintain
the majority of our regular school activities. That was one fantastic
shooting schedule. The timing was such that being on *SBTB* was
like an awesome summer job during high school that let me earn
and save money that would be there for college and later. Incredibly, even as I began to earn more, my parents never asked me for a

cent. I knew kids in the business whose parents spent all their money, because they thought they deserved it. Not my parents. They didn't want me to go crazy and spend all my money either. When it was time to buy a car, I used some of my earnings to buy a '65 Mustang, a junker. Dad and I worked together to fix it up, rebuilding the engine, putting in a new interior and dash, and painting it a fire engine red. If I had to do it over again, I would have gone with black, but that red Mustang was still cherry.

Even as *SBTB* garnered a bigger and bigger following, Chula kids didn't treat me that differently. I rarely brought up the Hollywood part of my life.

If someone said something, I'd say, "Oh, yeah, a kids' show. Whatever . . ." I did my best to downplay it. Because if I *didn't* act like it was no big deal, I probably would have gotten my ass kicked. As a wrestler on a high school team that was gunning to win the state title, being on TV added a challenge to matches—the last thing any wrestling competitor wanted to do was lose against some kid on a Saturday morning sitcom. So my opponents went at me hard. Well, I guess that forced me to go even harder. The state championship loomed large and I wasn't going to lose the chance to finish high school with that dream in hand.

The balancing act was nothing new. I mean, other than dating the girl of every high school guy's dreams and working on a hit TV show, the years when I was on *Saved by the Bell* were as close to normal as they could be. But to be honest, there were times when I felt like I was leading a double life. Only my fellow *SBTB* castmates knew that feeling, one I couldn't share with my friends at home. But only my Chula Vista friends and family knew the real, down-to-earth me. Both worlds were normal when taken separately, but living in both at the same time could get pretty bizarre.

•  •  •

*SBTB* was popular immediately but the show didn't hit its true stride until later, when we went into syndication, with episodes airing continuously for years by stations across the country and around the world. *Saved by the Bell* was to become a classic.

We did *SBTB* for five years and it ran all the way to 1994. The show ran, I ran, we all ran. It was magic. I never got bored. An irony of this show was that our executive producer, Peter Engel, wanted *SBTB* to be very squeaky clean and idealistic. Real high school is never anything like what you see on TV. What you see on TV is so sterile and safe. That's why on one of the episodes Artie the chameleon died, rather than a dog or a person. I was supposed to be distraught over a *lizard* dying? How was I supposed to drum up emotions for a little creature that ate flies and just moved his eyes in opposite directions? Originally, it was supposed to be a puppy that died, but Engel thought the puppy story line would have been too devastating for kids in our audience, so they changed it to a chameleon. Yet even that story line seemed to resonate— don't ask me why.

After *SBTB* ran its course, as the characters grew up, we would eventually do a season of the prime-time version, *Saved by the Bell: The College Years*. But our super conservative network executives were reluctant to get edgier for prime time, so the show ultimately didn't work. People couldn't suspend their disbelief that college life was so squeaky clean—it caused too much dissonance. Especially with our longtime fans.

In hindsight, I often marvel at how special it was to have an audience that grew up right along with us. I remember the shock of getting out and first meeting fans our age when we used to do live promotions in the early seasons of *SBTB*. These meet-and-greets were typically held in shopping malls and set up like rock concerts. Thousands of kids would show up to see us. The first time we did one of these, I knew the turnout would be enthusiastic, but nothing had prepared me for the crowds and the volume of the screaming from (mostly) girls when we stepped out onto the makeshift stage in the middle of their local mall.

That appearance was the first time that the girl fans came so close that they managed to slip me pieces of paper with their phone numbers; before I could react, their mothers did the same, slipping me their phone number with a quick hug and a hand in my pocket. At other mall promotions for the show, girls and/or moms would approach and shake my hand and the phone number would be in their palm, as if I was getting greased with some money. Other times, fans would ask me to sign a picture and as I was signing they would hand me an envelope with their phone number tucked inside. Sometimes girls would follow me around in public, even when I was just walking down the street out on an errand. In these days of twenty-four/seven entertainment news and paparazzi everywhere, that may not sound so crazy, but nothing really prepares you to have total strangers feel like they know you because you visit their living room every Saturday morning on the TV.

All that girl attention, I should add, was not terrible. I used to ask myself, Who wouldn't want thousands of girls screaming at you and saying how cute you are? The whole crazed-fan scene can also become commonplace, so that when you don't have it you begin to wonder whether you've lost your mojo. So I tried to enjoy the theatrics, even to the point of being fascinated by how far a girl or a mom would go to be with one of us guys in the cast.

Then there were the big car show promotions the network also had us doing. Car industrials can be like Las Vegas productions with carmakers bringing in their new cars of the new season or hosting classic car shows. As *SBTB* became more and more popular, I started getting opportunities to do personal appearances on my own, where they pay you to come hang out, sign autographs, and take pictures with people for a couple of hours. How cool! I could travel, I loved cars, and I was able to bring a friend or two with me. There were also lots of other people I might meet, like WWF wrestlers or soap opera stars.

Later on, I was fortunate enough to go to Europe for the first time because of the show—to France and England for promotional appearances—and to travel more all over the United States. For a kid from Chula Vista, the world was opening unbelievably wide for me in ways I never would have dreamt. The show was huge in France. To this day, French people will come up to me and say, *"Sauvés par le gong."* It was huge in Latin countries too: *"Salvados por la campana."* I loved the way they dubbed my voice in French and in Spanish because they gave me a really deep voice. Like Barry White. *"Y dónde está Screech?"* sounded pretty intense in that voice.

We were in Europe once for a sitcom awards festival similar to the Cannes Film Festival, also in the south of France. We stayed at the Hôtel Martinez, a fancy hotel that seemed fit for Louis XIV. Everything about that high life was intoxicating, especially the day we went to the beach. Wow, I'll never forget seeing topless women out on the beach for the first time.

You would think that my understanding of the opposite sex and of relationships would have been much more sophisticated by the time I was in my late teens and after being exposed to so much attention. Not so. As only the events of my earlier adolescent years reveal, I grew up very much in the throes of fast times at Chula Vista High.

# CHAPTER 4
## *MI VIDA LOCA*

Yes, the rumors are true: I love women and have always been fascinated by them, from as far back as I can remember. But I should clarify that I've never been the kind of guy who likes to think of himself as a player. That implies that you're playing a game or that you're out to trick a girl. That's never been me. My feeling is that if you are up-front about the attraction and if it's mutual, it's honest and sexy at the same time. But, of course, romantic relationships can become much more complicated than that. Why? Well, for starters, as I learned from many mistakes when I was young and, in some cases, at times when I was commitment averse, not everybody is comfortable with the "love the one you're with" approach. Also—and this is partly what fascinates me about them—most women are complicated.

If I could sum up everything I know now that I really wish I would have known back when I was young and single, it's this simple fact: women don't want you to be a superhero and fix all their problems; they just want you to listen. Younger guys always ask me to dole out secrets to scoring with girls, and, honestly, that's all I got. But it's million-dollar advice: just be a good listener.

It took me a long time to learn that, and much of what I now know about the opposite sex would come later on when, appropriately, I had more serious relationships. But in the meantime, from the moment I hit puberty, I couldn't wait to get the lowdown, especially because it seemed to be the number one topic of conversation for my older cousins. Some of them, in their midteens when I was turning thirteen, had lost their virginity at fourteen or even younger. So, for me, listening to them recount their conquests convinced me they had to be experts. Or maybe it was just all that sex talk, combined with my newly sprouted hormones, that got me really interested in whatever advice they could offer.

For example, my cousin Victor once told a story about someone he knew who was in bed with a girl and couldn't perform. "What was wrong with him?" another cousin asked.

"Alcohol," Victor said, explaining that too much booze could hamper performance.

I knew almost nothing about the mechanics of sex, but that struck a chord with me. Sure enough, I later learned firsthand that if you plan on being good in bed, don't drink too much beforehand. Not rocket science, but good to remember.

My expectations may have been too high on the kind of wisdom they could give me. In hindsight, I realize it was unlikely that I could learn anything valuable about sex and girls from slightly older cousins who were as hormonally crazed as me. This is not to say that my cousins steered me wrong completely. However, none of them were by any means experts in sex education and I had no other sources of reliable information. No nudie magazines left lying around or even boring scientific guides. There was definitely nothing in school early on, like health class in high school would later provide. With my cousins, I did get a lot of slang for sex and heard all kinds of curse words—in English and Spanish—but since I personally was never much of a cursing type, that was just like color commentary about sports. No cautionary tales about things like how to use a condom or anything about birth control at all.

Even basic questions I put to the guys, such as, "How do you know if a girl likes you?" were answered with a total lack of expertise.

In that instance, back when I was about ten years old, one of my cousins said, "Girls like dimples." In some ways, that was all I needed to know.

Up until that moment, my dimples had been the butt of constant jokes.

My adult relatives, like my various *tías*, were different. "Oh, Mario, where did you get your dimples? They are so adorable!"

Some of them actually knew the answer, that I inherited dimples from Dad's side of the family. He has a dimpled chin and one on his left cheek; later on, when Marissa married and had babies, her daughter, my niece Kalia, would have a dimple as well.

Kids at school never told me that dimples were cool. They used to say, "Oh, you got holes in your face!" Holes in my face? Little kids in Chula could be tough. Or, because my dimples are really pretty deep, they'd call me "Pitface."

For all those years, if you want to know the truth, I was embarrassed enough by my dimples that I'd try not to smile too often. So you can imagine my shock to discover that girls thought dimples were cute. After that revelation, I started not to mind them as much.

The tag to this anecdote is that many years later, as an adult, I was surprised to learn that dimples are actually birth defects. Turns out that dimples are a fatigue of the muscles that never really developed in the face, thereby creating a small cavity. No, mine aren't small. They're like the Grand Canyon of dimples. Some people just have small lines, like Tom Selleck, or tiny nicks, like Beyoncé, but mine are more akin to cereal bowls. That said, birth defects and all, dimples did seem to work in my favor. Lesson in point: sometimes the physical traits you obsess over can turn out to be a blessing.

But as for the advice about what made girls like boys, when I was in the fifth grade and developed my first real crush on a girl named Sherry, I needed something more concrete than just having dimples. This was before the first kiss that I would share with Fergie aka Stacy Ferguson on *Kids Incorporated*, and I was convinced that Sherry didn't know I was alive. She was a year or more ahead of me in school and—I'm not kidding—every time I was lucky enough to see her in passing, she took my breath away. So beautiful, Sherry was exotic looking with long dark hair and big brown eyes. Oh, and she was a twin. As a red-blooded all-American kid of Latino descent, I came to the conclusion that there could be nothing sexier than twins—two identically beautiful girls. But Sherry had that extra something, a spark that made her stand out. I was so enamored with her that I was too nervous to even go up to say hello.

Cousin Victor pointed out, "You have the gift of gab, man. What's the problem?"

He was right. I was usually comfortable talking to everyone. But Sherry was so unattainable, partly because she was older and those age gaps do seem wider when you're a child. Young and in love though I was, every time I had the chance to approach her, I became anxious and shy and overly self-conscious, worrying about what she would see in a fifth-grade peon like me. My answer? Nothing. Clearly, I was destined to appreciate her from afar. Every single love song that came on the radio—especially anything by Hall and Oates, the best singing duo of all time—and I'd mourn the loss of what never could be. But soon enough I forced myself to forget about Sherry.

Probably it was at that point that I decided to try caring a little less and borrow some of the cool that helped me in the audition process. By the time I was twelve, I had enjoyed a few more fun flirtations along the lines of my behind-the-scenes kissing with Fergie. Without any guidance from my cousins, I found out that, along with being cool, if I was just myself, girls liked that. The other eye-opener was finding out that when the chemistry is there, nature usually takes its course. For example, at a dance competition when I was in the seventh grade, I sensed mutual sparks with Gina Giacinto, a gorgeous dancer of Italian descent who would later be crowned Miss Nevada, a real beauty queen. The flirtation was like a dance. With no deliberate agenda on my part, we ended up behind the dance studio alone, making out.

After that, I became a bit of a natural with girls—maybe a little too natural. What do I mean? Well, when you are in the eighth grade and it's the day before your thirteenth birthday and you are alone for the first time with the sweet young beauty, letting nature take its course is not always advisable.

At this point, my sixteen- and seventeen-year-old cousins— also wrestlers—had yet to offer any specifics about how to advance from first to second base and so on. They talked like sex pros, but the whole process was still a mystery to me and I was gung ho to find out what the real deal was. Without question, hoping to go all the way with a girl at thirteen is too young, although no one in my circle was around to say so. Granted, everyone grows up fast in the hood. Too fast, if you ask me. Back then, though, given my surging hormones, I was not only curious but at the age of wanting to keep up and impress my cousins and neighborhood friends.

Keep in mind that back in those days I did not appear to be your normal preteen. By the time I was about twelve, I looked like a little man-boy, like I was sixteen or seventeen, not twelve going on thirteen. In addition to wrestling all this time, I ate well and had already started lifting, so I had muscles. No doubt about it, I had a teenager's body. Of course, I still had the maturity of a thirteen-year-old.

But compared to how intimidated I was with Sherry, I was practically Don Juan when it came to breaking the ice with my next serious crush, Gina, a pretty, soulful gymnast who went to a neighboring school. Natural as can be, I walked right up to her on the football field after a big Friday night football game and introduced myself. She nodded with a little questioning look in her eyes. It took big cojones to approach a girl from the opposing side. Then I asked her out. She said, "Okay," and, cool as a cucumber, I gave her a smile and told her I'd get back to her with details.

Gina was two or three years older than me, half Greek and exotic looking in a potentially smoldering way. And hard of hearing—as she put it. Her impairment meant that she could talk a little but not very well. I remember when Gina called me we used this service for the hearing-impaired that involved a live operator on the call to translate. The operator would type whatever I said so Gina could read it on a display she had on her phone; for me, the operator would simply repeat everything Gina said so that I could understand. The operator might repeat by interjecting, "She says she really misses you. She says she can't wait to see you." She would then key in whatever I replied, verbatim, and we would converse that way over the phone.

Sometimes it was weird to flirt over the phone with a detached translator. Just to push the envelope and get Gina to laugh, I decided to mess with the operator one evening and said to tell Gina, "The body's in the trunk, but I'm going to get rid of it as soon as possible." There was a long pause on the other end. Finally, I broke out laughing and said, "I'm kidding, I'm kidding."

When I explained this to Gina, she thought that was hilarious. For those who are taking notes, girls do seem to like guys who have a good sense of humor. I should add that Gina and I were never officially dating. I was only thirteen and what we had was more like a flirtatious affair or juvenile infatuation. An amazing girl, Gina and I stayed friends all the way through high school. And even to this day, I sometimes still run into her—she is now married with kids and is still a beauty.

There was never much of an opportunity to take our flirtation to the next level until one day when the rest of my family happened to be away visiting a relative and I realized that I would have the house to myself. After inviting her over, she arrived in record time. We started to kiss on the living room sofa and then became more physical. But then, thinking ahead—at least at that stage—we moved to the floor closer to an exit, in case I heard anyone coming home. That way, if our clothes came off, we could put them back on in a hurry and escape.

What happened next was mostly a blur. I remember a lot of kissing and touching, but past that, I was clueless. I knew nothing about a woman's body. All I could do was try desperately to piece together the fragmented and unreliable information that I'd heard from my older cousins and kick myself for never asking specific questions. The hotter and heavier it got, the less sure I was about what went where. For crying out loud, I was way off the mark!

When I later talked to Cousin Victor, I asked him how guys knew what to do the first time they went all the way and he said, "Let me spell it out, man. If you wanted to put a key in the lock on a front door, you kinda figure it out." Yeah, well, before I figured it out, I was about two inches above that.

Even though I wasn't suave in the least, as nature did take its course, Gina and I were still so into each other. Her hair smelled incredible and her skin was so soft. We were both a little slick from perspiration and nerves—this was a first time for both of us. The blind leading the blind?

To tell you the truth, I don't know how making out and heavy petting got us to the point of having sex. We hadn't fooled around that much before that fateful day, but it just happened—right at the moment that I was about to give up. Eureka! My eyes rolled back and I could not believe what I was feeling. Euphoria! Nothing like anything I'd ever felt before. Klondike bars, my favorite dessert, have nothing on losing your virginity.

The reality check slammed me and Gina about five minutes after we were dressed. We were so caught up in figuring out what to do that I didn't even use a condom! Which is crazy at any age, never mind at twelve years old. Much as I would like to excuse myself, I knew better. I'm not an absolute idiot. Even though I knew very little about sex, I knew enough about reproduction to have acted more responsibly. I knew that if I was old enough to have an orgasm, I was old enough to have babies. Can you imagine? At this writing, I could have a son or daughter in his or her thirties—or even be a grandfather! It would have been helpful if my cousins had gone over the issue of birth control more when they were talking about their sexual experiences.

What's a twelve-, almost-thirteen-year-old kid to do in this situation? Later that night, I called my cousin Victor, whispering so no one could overhear, as I told him what happened. That was when he gave me the key-in-lock analogy.

"But I didn't use a condom," I went on. "What do we do?!"

"Well, did you pull out?" Victor almost screamed what hardly sounded like a question.

"What is that? What do you mean, 'pull out'?"

He was laughing, but I didn't think it was funny at all, even though he was trying to be as supportive as he could. At fifteen, he was also the only person I could trust to give me answers to hopefully alleviate my anxiety. Finally, he said, "Well, Mario, it's too late now—no sense stressing out over it. You'll have to just wait to find out."

Waiting for those next thirty days was torture for me and Gina. What would we do if she was pregnant and we had to raise a child? We didn't even talk about it, other than staying glued to a menstrual calendar and praying that she got her period.

The day she told me we were in the clear, I literally jumped up and down. You would think that I would have learned a valuable lifelong lesson right there and then, but no. It's very true: hormones rule the mind of a young teen. They rule everything. Or so it was with me. And once I had sex, I was hooked. As time went on, I'd say that sex became my drug of choice, as addictive as the strongest stuff out there. In most respects, I was Mr. Clean, staying away from drugs and out of any serious trouble. But when it came to sex, I might as well have been a junkie.

So Gina and I continued having sex and I continued not to wear condoms, telling myself that pulling out in time would get the job done. Luckily, she and I never had a close call after that first time, but that doesn't make me any less stupid. Much to my embarrassment these many years later, I look back now and realize how ridiculous it was to have taken those chances and to remain so ignorant.

True, my parents had never sat me down and given me the sex talk. If I had gone to Mom, she would have openly discussed the realities and given me some guidance; I felt comfortable enough telling her pretty much anything. My dad was another story. The closest I got to having "the talk" with my father didn't happen until 1990, when I was almost seventeen and the news broke that Magic Johnson had HIV. Everybody freaked out because of the lack of awareness about the virus in all communities and how it could be spread through unprotected sex. As it should have, Magic's announcement made knowledge of safe sex a life-and-death issue.

My dad was concerned and I know that his intention was to come to me with all of his tender father-son emotions bubbling over. Instead, he sat me down and was very cut-and-dried. "Hey, *mijo*," he began. "You know, there's a lot of that AIDS stuff going around right now. So, you know, if you're going to do anything with, like, a girl or anything, just, ah, you know, put something on it." And then he stood up and gave me an affirming "Job well done" slap on the back and walked into the kitchen to get a beer.

That was it, unfortunately. No eye contact, no sensitive questions asked. My father did make some good points over the years, but usually we didn't talk about intimacy issues. I could ask him for relationship advice and he'd go on and on about that, but when it came to sex, he'd just close up shop.

The truth is, I was really lucky to come of age when I did and to experience a sexual awakening with a girl as special as Gina. And even with lots more to learn in the love and sex departments, I knew how lucky I was, especially compared to some of my friends. But my luck was about to run out.

"Oh, hey, Mario. Nice to meet ya," said the cute girl with the pronounced Southern accent who caught my eye back in early 1989.

I was fifteen at the time and Chula Vista's wrestling team had gone to compete against another local high school. What stands out in my memory of this day is the echo of "Welcome to the Jungle" by Guns N' Roses. At wrestling meets, that song was how our team was introduced, as the announcer would say, "Let's hear it for the Chula Vista High School Spartans!" We'd hear the guitar, *dah dah dah dah dah dah* . . . and the hook, "You're in the jungle, baby!" followed by, "You're gonna die!" and then we'd come out. That whole Guns N' Roses album, *Appetite for Destruction*, was a sound track for my wrestling days, always pumping me up before a meet.

Known as a popular kid, I was having a great year, thanks to wrestling and other sports, as well as academics and various extra-curricular activities. I definitely was enjoying the advantages of being popular and was still in the throes of high-octane hormones.

Sex is, after all, such a natural part of being human, and I had so much appreciation for the young ladies at this stage that I had begun to accept aspects of *la vida loca* as part of who I was—an extremely sexual being. Maybe some of my drive was a form of re-bellion, a way to be a bad boy, kind of, when I was basically so hardworking with my career and my schooling. Who knows? Again, I really had no teenage vices. Drugs were taboo for me and I didn't even smoke. In my mind, if rock 'n' rollers could have their addictions, I could have this pure and crystal clear interest in the opposite sex. Back in the day, Adam Ant had a song that asked if you didn't drink and didn't smoke, "what do you do?"

In that stage of my teenage years, fueled by this crazy drive that had only begun to kick into higher gear, I was about to make one of the most painful mistakes of my young life. I'm blessed that the young woman in question was mature enough to make the dif-ficult choice when we were both too young and too irresponsible to plan ahead.

Her name, she told me that day, over the fading refrain of "Welcome to the Jungle," was Patty Lynn. She was my age, and was the assistant to our athletic trainer at the high school, a precur-sor to what she was sure would be a big career in sports medicine.

Boy oh boy, was she hot. And charming. And soon enough, I heard a sweet Texas drawl. With a name like Patty Lynn, I guessed she would have to be from somewhere below the Mason-Dixon Line.

After introducing myself at the meet, I asked for her phone number and we started hanging out, immediately discovering that our infatuation was mutual. But we took it slow, relatively speaking. Then, after five or six months of being inseparable and caught up in our puppy love, we started sleeping together.

Had I listened and learned from the mistakes of others, I would have known better than to believe the lie that I could pull out in time in the throes of passion. Because sometimes you can't and don't. Or other times you and your girlfriend have those moments where you think it's the right time of the month so you don't have to worry. But that's a real recipe for trouble.

That mind-set is not unlike Russian roulette—if you play long enough, eventually one of the bullets will find its mark. Unless you are smart or not so cavalier, you end up making a mistake you can't undo.

Patty Lynn waited until she had been to the doctor before calling to give me the news that she was pregnant. The phone conversation was not easy, to say the least. She didn't cry, but I think she was still too stunned to be overly emotional. Now that I saw the consequences of my actions, I was ready to make whatever sacrifices were asked of me. My mind raced with what this was going to entail: we'd get married, I'd help raise the baby, quit acting to get a real job, possibly drop out of school.

"No, Mario," Patty Lynn stopped me. She was one hundred percent certain that she didn't want to have the baby and was adamant about taking care of terminating the pregnancy right way. This had to be her choice; that much I knew. And I accepted that this was the best decision for her, and probably for me too. But between my guilt at getting us into this predicament and the disappointment I knew my mom would have in me, I was devastated.

At first, I did all I could to avoid Mom finding out. But it turned out that I couldn't access my savings on my own. Even though I had money saved from my years of working, I couldn't just withdraw it from the bank because of safeguards put in place early on to prevent anyone from using funds that were supposed to be for my future. Then I tried to borrow the money so no one would find out. But I was a kid who had money so everyone I asked—a few of my cousins, my uncle, a few friends—thought I was being greedy or off on some wild venture. The whole thing was suspicious. And of course, my mom caught wind that I was trying to borrow money.

Mortified and scared, I went to my mother and first explained that Patty Lynn had made her choice and I was going to support that choice. At that point, I could have denied what was happening, but I had to man up. After I told her that it was my responsibility and I was never going to let it happen again, I went down on my knees to ask for forgiveness. If there had been a possibility that Patty Lynn and I were in love or had a desire for commitment, maybe we could have found another way, but the truth was that we had no business bringing a baby into the world. We were babies ourselves.

My mother believed how contrite I truly was and knew that the mistake I owned had already cost me emotionally, spiritually, and now financially. She could have berated me, but by then it was pretty clear that I was doing a good job of that on my own. Mom asked me just to make sure this was what Patty Lynn wanted.

In fact it was and I always would respect her decision. After our ordeal, Patty Lynn seemed more relieved than anything and we came out of it better friends than we had been before. A short time later we went our separate ways without any wrenching breakup or good-bye.

When you're young and you make a mistake, it can feel like the end of the world. Time does have a way of healing the wounds. We both moved on and life brought other ordeals and other joys. Sometimes I still think about it all and wonder if she had any children, if she's married now. What if I had married her after all or if she had changed her mind? What would that child be like and how would the rest of my life have been different? In those moments, a chill runs through my body and I try to shake the thought from my head. Patty Lynn made her choice. It was always hers to make. Sure, I could have tried to stop her, but I chose to respect her choice and our mutual decision that we weren't ready to be parents.

As time has passed and I've matured, I have wrestled with the mistake that I made out of arrogance, among other missteps I've made over the years, and I've spent many a night awake thinking how I could have done things differently. Obviously, I can't change the fact that I was a reckless, horny kid. I wish it were different. Like everyone else, I've struggled with my demons and work toward a better me every day. I will say this: I've tried to embrace my responsibilities and have chosen not to be in denial or run away from problems. As someone who was always a gentleman with girls, I know that it was right to leave the choice of how to face an unwanted pregnancy up to her completely, and to be there to support her.

For a few months after Patty Lynn and I broke it off, I decided to try to cool it with girls for a while. But then, wouldn't you know it, for the first time ever a woman entered my life and I fell seriously in love.

Now I was really in for trouble.

• • •

What is it about me and gorgeous Italian girls? Not to throw out a spoiler or anything, but when everything happened with Monica it was not the first or the last time that I was to fall in love with a beautiful dancer of Italian descent.

"In love?" my cousin Victor teased me. "You know you just fall in lust. It'll pass."

"You know how I know?" I remember saying. "Because I don't care about anything else!"

This was around the time that I was auditioning for *Saved by the Bell* and it may have had something to do with my not trying too hard on those calls. All I could think about was Monica. Did it matter that I was fifteen and she was nineteen? Not to me, but that's a significant difference in age. She may as well have been thirty-five for how much more experienced she was than me. Monica was one of my dance teachers at a studio in San Diego, about thirty minutes north of Chula Vista, where I studied off and on. Monica and I casually started messing around, and continued from there. She was definitely a woman, not a girl—with a beautiful dancer's body, curvy and strong. All real woman.

I was obsessed with everything about her. At nineteen, she was an experienced young woman, she was sexy, she was talented, and she was my dance teacher. Fantasy come true? But acting on it wasn't a plan. Basically, I had started taking lessons from her a couple of years earlier, long before anything happened. One day, she invited me to a party at her house with various friends and family connected to the studio. We started talking and she knew I had a crush on her. Maybe I grabbed her hand under the table and then we started flirting. Soon after, we were a thing. Once we started, like a drug addict, I couldn't stop. The sex was unbelievable. We did it everywhere, in the car, in the studio, on the mats that we'd pull out for cushioning.

Certainly, I'd been on the rampaging-hormones craze before. But this was amplified by the conviction that there was no one I was ever going to love as much as Monica. How crazed was I? Just to spend extra time with her, I started ditching school and wrestling practice. Me? The guy who was determined to get my team in contention to compete for the title? Dad suspected trouble and began to send his brother, my uncle Tavo, over to the gym to make sure I had been at school and was at practice.

One day, when I was skipping school, I took my '65 Mustang—which I had only just gotten licensed to drive—to go see Monica. On the way there, I parked in front of the 7-Eleven, dashed in to buy some mints or something, and then when I got back in the car, Uncle Tavo popped up out of the backseat!

"What are you doing?!" I just about jumped out of my pants.

He told me what was what, that I was going to mess up my life if I kept on this path. But luckily he didn't tell on me. Not so luckily, I got a speeding ticket coming home from Monica's house.

Even the cousins started to worry about me. Victor warned, "You gotta get ahold of yourself, man."

He was right. I was so infatuated with this woman, whatever she'd tell me to do, I would do. If she had asked, I probably would have crawled to her house on all fours. Not that she would have asked. Monica was really a sweetheart. It was almost as if some witch doctor had slipped me a potion.

My mom and dad became concerned at how distracted I was, what with ditching school and practice. That was unlike me. In an attempt to be diplomatic, my parents cautioned me to slow down because, God forbid, I could get Monica pregnant or something bad could happen. Besides, they reminded me about the auditions under way and how a serious relationship could hurt my being cast in general, not to mention that if I still wanted to go to college to wrestle, the fact that my grades were suffering at school could come back to haunt me.

This was the most animated I'd seen my dad become about who I was dating. Of course, throughout my upbringing and even later, my father had very strong opinions about who was and wasn't trustworthy. Dad never held back from telling me which of my friends, in his words, were a worthless piece of you know what. He had no patience for freeloaders. You couldn't come over to my house and spend the night more than twice and eat his food more than one day in a row or he'd start putting you to work to earn your keep. In retrospect, I think because of his keen eye for others who tried to pull something over or were phony in any way, I would go on to fine-tune my own instincts for who was a true friend and who was just out for a free ride. In show business, that was going to be especially important—whether it came to agents, managers, and other business representatives or to the usual hangers-on and people who gravitate toward the success of others and try to take advantage. Both of my parents are good judges of character and I like to think they passed that torch to me.

But at this time in my all-consuming passion with Monica, I was in full-on "parents just don't understand" mode. I didn't want their judgment, warnings, or interference. The more they showed their concern, the more resentful I became.

Everything came to a head one day when my dad answered the phone as I was about to pick it up, knowing it was Monica calling for me.

Without so much as consulting me, he said, "Hey, I don't want you calling here anymore. That's it—my son's not going to talk to you anymore." And he hung up.

"Dad!" I bellowed like a wounded animal. "Why did you do that?! What's your problem?" It was the first time I ever talked back to my dad.

To my father's credit, he saw instantly that I was really in love with her. "Whoa," he began, taking his time. "You are serious, aren't you?" He and I had a man-to-man argument and he conceded that he understood where I was coming from. But in the end, he made it clear that it couldn't go on. His word was the law.

I was heartbroken, beyond comfort. What could I do? I shed tears, no question, but they were mostly tears of anger. Sad and conflicted, I obeyed my father's edict. But I believed at the time it was cruel and unfair. Now, years later, I see that it was probably the best thing that could have happened. Dad did me a favor. In the state I was in, I quite possibly could have tried to marry Monica, gotten her pregnant, and my career would have stopped short.

Don't get me wrong—I didn't take it lying down. I kept seeing her behind their backs until she put a stop to that. I even tried toilet-papering her house, because nothing says "I love you" like draping toilet paper from the trees of your lost lover's front yard, roof, and down the walls of her house. Any excuse to be near her or to have her attentions, even in negative ways, I'd use. These didn't ease the pain, not surprisingly. And in the end, although I recovered, part of me would always be filled with remorse— because we never said good-bye, and then I never saw her again.

Not to put too fine a point on it, but as you now know, when the opportunity came along for me to be cast on a groundbreaking popular TV series at such a tumultuous time in my young life, I really was saved by the bell! The timing was ideal for getting over all that teenage angst and going back to savoring all the opportunities and experiences that my crazy life kept serving up for me.

*Saved by the Bell* had just finished airing its second season when my high school graduation rolled around in early summer 1991. The Spartans wrestling team had made a name for ourselves in San Diego and on the state level. Individually, I placed among the top wrestlers in the state my two last years of high school, placing seventh overall in the state of California high school rankings my senior year. Not too shabby. In keeping with our local nickname of "Sexy Town," the Chula Vista High School theme song for senior prom was "I Wanna Sex You Up," by Color Me Badd.

You think I'm making that up? I laugh just remembering how we all loved that song and how we went nuts dancing to it at prom. And, actually, that song holds up to this day. It's hot and sexy, and so groovy.

A month before graduation I'd confronted probably the biggest decision of my life until then. Ever since I was ten years old, it was implicit that I was working as a child actor to save money for my future—specifically, that is, for college. My parents couldn't afford to send me to college without my help. But that was the plan. If I dug into my savings and was able to earn a wrestling scholarship too, I could pay for myself and fulfill the dream of being the first in our family to go to college. Sure enough, I was offered scholarships from a few schools—Arizona State, University of Minnesota, some of the California state schools.

"But you know," I explained to Mom, "I have a job on TV that I love. What's the point of quitting to go to college to earn a degree to do something else?"

"You're right, *mijo*. You are working. You already have a career, if that's what you want to do."

Initially, I resolved to do both: go to college and continue working as an actor. Given the production schedule for *SBTB*, I could pull that off. And I'm very proud to say that among my top choices, I was accepted to UCLA, Pepperdine, and Loyola Marymount. Wow. That was no small achievement in my eyes. Somehow, between having good grades and the admissions advantage of my Mexican background, I was given a chance to walk through the doors at some of California's top educational institutions.

At the same time, I couldn't get the thought out of my head that I was already working in the entertainment industry on a regular series in a role that others could only dream of having. All these years, I'd lived a double life, balancing showbiz with school. Now, suddenly, where once acting had been a means to the end, I began to consider that it was the end—or what I really wanted to do after all.

My parents supported me one hundred percent. As I promised, if acting slowed down, I could always go back to college. But while I was thriving in my field, why not focus on that and see where opportunities led? The plan was to focus on acting for the time being and then later on school—in other words, one thing at a time. As a family, we were seasoned enough to know that a career in entertainment might be short-lived. No one said it at the time but as smart and on the ball as Marissa was, if I didn't make it to college, she was certainly on her way. And yes, my sister was going to carry that banner as the first in the family to go to college and make us all proud.

Once the decision had been made, I went to work that same summer to shoot our next season for *Saved by the Bell*. One day on the set during a blocking rehearsal, I looked around and nodded to myself. What was I ever in doubt over? I loved being an actor. Taking nothing for granted, I was going to work harder than ever, harder than anyone I knew. So much would depend on forces outside my control and on how lucky I continued to be. But one thing was clear to me: this was where I was supposed to be all along.

Mom and Dad gave me their full blessing. If I hadn't still been shooting *Saved by the Bell* or if the show had ended early for whatever reason, I would have jumped right into college. But trying to do both and do them both well wasn't a viable plan. So I chose my career and never looked back. And even with many life lessons still to learn, I'm grateful to say that my luck never did run out.

# CHAPTER 5

# LIFE AFTER
# A. C. SLATER

When I made the decision to become a serious business investor, I'd just turned nineteen years old and was coming up on my last year of working on *Saved by the Bell*. This wasn't the end of the ride necessarily, as there was talk of a series sequel that would move us high school students into our college years. We also could look forward to some fun reunion specials to be shot on location in places like Hawaii and Las Vegas. Not only would those projects extend the *SBTB* franchise and, thus, the life of A. C. Slater, but also, thanks to an anticipated syndication deal, we'd be earning that many more royalty checks from reruns.

Sweet! Little did I know that *Saved by the Bell* would come to occupy a rare space in syndication heaven—airing every day, all over the world, in more than 163 countries. And even at this writing, it's *still* rerunning, twenty-five years after *SBTB* debuted as a kids' show on Saturday mornings! Knowing what I do now, the number one item on my list of things I wish I'd known back then is that I should have negotiated a better contract for these reruns. No lie, I receive residual checks that are worth less than the postage on the envelope they're mailed in.

At age nineteen, however, I didn't have that kind of foresight. What I did have was a sense of the hurdles I would face in finding my next viable acting role after the series ended—especially after becoming so recognizable as Slater. Five years of playing the same character can cement those images into the public's mind and, more to the point, in the minds of producers looking to hire actors. With that starting to weigh on my awareness, I thought it would be smart to put on my business hat and explore possible investment ventures beyond the world of showbiz. After turning eighteen, I had finally been given access to all that money that I'd saved over the years as a child actor. The first move I made was to leave my childhood home in Chula Vista and relocate to Hollywood full-time in my own apartment as a self-supporting actor. After that, it made sense to look for ways that my earnings could go to work for me, even before the series came to a close. Right? And, lo and behold, one of the first opportunities to come along when I was nineteen seemed like a no-brainer.

"Mario, if you're seriously thinking about investing in a real business, I have a possibility that might interest you . . ." was how the owner of Mr. Crowns, one of the hottest joints in Tijuana, first raised the suggestion.

Back in the 1990s, down in San Diego all of us American kids in our late teens and twenties knew all about Mr. Crowns and the wild, fun-filled nightlife to be found just across the border in Tijuana. Again, crossing the border was nothing back in the decade before September 11, 2001, and the main party destination on the Mexican side was Avenida Revolución. Every single spot on Revolución was a nightclub or bar, all of them featuring crazy drink specials and a young American crowd. There was Rio Rita, Señor Frog's, Escape, House, and more. Like Bourbon Street in New Orleans, the street's whole ambience was a crazy youth- and alcohol-driven scene. You'd see all stages of uninhibited partying—from make-out sessions in public to girls throwing up in the streets, even dropping their pants to pee right in the parking lot.

American kids flocked there because the legal drinking age was eighteen, not twenty-one as it is in the States. Actually, a lot of us started going down to Avenida Revolución even earlier, like at fifteen or sixteen. Everyone knew that the doormen weren't exactly enforcing a strict ID policy. In my opinion, eighteen is too young to drink like that, especially with the combination of drinking and driving. Thankfully, I was never that stupid. Never once in my life did I get behind the wheel of a car when I was drunk, not even a little bit. Never. Unfortunately there were those who did, and as a result that corridor along the Mexico-U.S. border was a dangerous place in the hours between nine p.m. and six a.m. Every now and then, someone did get hit in the road.

For the most part, though, a foray to Revolución was a fun, fun time. Bars didn't close until six in the morning and the only reason they did was so the staff could clean up and restock. The mentality for many people, not so different from today, was that you could visit another country and become someone else. Tourists would leave their inhibitions, and even their morals, back in the States. Girls were naughty and guys went out of their minds. Imagine how drunk you could get on five-dollar all-you-can-drink beer nights.

Mr. Crowns, named after the owner, Tommy Corona (*corona* means "crown" in Spanish), was my destination of choice. The bar was right on the corner of Calle Sexta (Sixth Street) and Avenida Revolución, a total hot spot. It was sort of an indoor/outdoor deal, with two floors and DJs on each of them. From the start, Tommy and I hit it off and became good friends. He was a kickboxer and a surfer, and despite the fact that he was ten years older than me, we had lots of interests in common. My group of friends tended to be older than me, so that was not unusual.

Though I don't remember how the subject of business investments came up, I was all ears when Tommy mentioned this oppor-tunity that seemed to have my name on it. Apparently, his lease on Mr. Crowns was about to be up, and after a falling-out with his existing investors (I probably should have looked into this piece of information more than I did), Tommy was planning to move Mr. Crowns to a new location on Revolución. Naturally, he was looking for new investors. In the past he'd usually brought his dad in on business ventures, but this time he wanted to go it alone, outside the family. What were we talking about? Well, for a $65,000 in-vestment, I could become ten percent owner.

Then and there, I couldn't think of a single reason why invest-ing in a bar, particularly on that street, would be a bad idea. Of course, I didn't know anything about bookkeeping or running a bar . . . but that didn't stop me. I said, "Why not?" and in I went with both feet.

Here's a spoiler alert: $65,000 is a lot of margaritas, my friends, and a really bad idea.

Mom, who had never steered me wrong, had a much more reasonable idea. She recommended that I buy my first house in-stead. Taking her advice, before I bought the bar, I bought a little house in Chula Vista, using it as a rental property. The house turned out to be a good investment, but not the bar. The bar was a stone-cold horrible investment.

My business plan and vetting process consisted of nothing more than an emotional inventory of experiences on Revolución. Why mistrust my own eyes? If the bars there were always crowded, how could I lose?

In the beginning I loved the creative part of designing the space and just the coolness of being a teenage owner of a bar. So what if I wasn't going to college? I was getting real-world experi-ence and I was thinking economically too. When I came up with the interior design I wanted to achieve, for example, my dad got involved, and using contacts at his job with National City—a neighboring town next to Chula Vista—he was able to help us find used traffic display items like stoplights and flashing "Don't Walk" signs. When we hung those, they gave the bar an authentic roughed-up nightlife look: dark atmosphere with strategic lighting, concrete floors, band posters on the walls. Later on, I was also responsible for developing "Mr. Crowns Presents," which involved booking and promoting a super cool concert in Rosarito Beach with top names: Faith No More and Perry Farrell (the former lead singer of Jane's Addiction) with his band Porno for Pyros. The process was not brain surgery; I called the agent and I booked the acts. Just like that, and it felt great.

For much of the time that I did own a piece of the bar, I had a blast. The girls, the booze, the fights, the drunks, and yes, the sex. Sometimes it felt like the Wild West. There were instances when it was so rowdy, you knew a fight was going to break out at any moment and you'd best stay out of the line of fire. That was the case on one occasion when, to paraphrase the words of Phil Collins, I could feel it coming in the air that night.

In those days, I had been dating the actress Jaime Pressly (from *My Name Is Earl* and *Joe Dirt*) for almost a year, though it wasn't a serious relationship. We'd met while filming a sci-fi flick called *The Journey: Absolution*, in which we played futuristic soldiers fighting off an alien invasion. Like a lot of "showmances," ours started because we worked well together and liked each other's company when we were off the clock. Jaime, an Emmy Award–winning actress and talented comedian, had driven down with me to San Diego a few times before—when we'd stay in my parents' guesthouse—and a couple of those times we'd gone to Tijuana together to check out the bar. Nothing wild had happened, even though she turned plenty of heads. Jaime has one of those striking faces you never forget at the same time that she has the classic blond all-American cheerleader look. Killer body, great smile, a lot of sass. Jaime had always been her own person—cool, beyond sexy, a sweet girl, and ready for adventure. We both loved to dance and, oh yeah, she knew how to move.

As I remember, Jaime and I headed down to the bar to have a few drinks and hang with some friends. But as soon as we walked in the door, I could tell the crowd was rowdier than usual. It was in the air. The bar was never a showplace for elegance, but on this particular occasion it had been trashed already, which was unusual for so early in the night. The stained concrete floor was covered with small puddles of cheap beer, shredded napkins, and cigarette butts, and you can imagine what it smelled like—discount perfume, smoke, sweat . . .

We sat at the bar with our crew, talking with friends, and ordered some drinks. Next thing I knew multiple fights began to break out. My policy at this stage was to stay as cool and collected as possible and to encourage that attitude in others. Sure enough, that approach seemed to calm everything down quickly. That was, until I caught sight of another eruption, this one involving a buddy of mine, Brady (who we called "Granny" because his last name was Granier). Basically a good-looking all-American guy from a Cajun background, Granny is one of the nicest guys in the world and would never intentionally get into a brawl. But it looked as if he had bumped into this other tough-looking guy by accident and then knocked over a drink. Something that innocent. A gentleman, Granny instantly apologized and was wholly charming about it. But the tough guy he'd disturbed wasn't in the mood to let it go. Suddenly, as I watched from near the front, the guy escalated the whole thing and started pushing Granny around, his fists clenched.

"Hey, man," I said, calling out the troublemaker as I went over to the two of them to intervene. "Let's squash this. Got it? Let's move on." The tough guy, eyes blazing, wouldn't drop it. I continued in an authoritative tone, "Listen, we don't need any of that. Let's just be cool."

I was trying to be a peacemaker. But this guy wasn't going to give in to me. Instead, he goes and gets lippy and then shoves me.

I tried again. "Chill out," I told him. That didn't work either. He started getting really aggressive and cursing at me as he raised his hand.

That's all it took to set off what was still sometimes a short fuse. In hindsight, I could have called the cops earlier, but in that moment, as a part owner and a wrestler, I just reacted—a knee-jerk reaction with a lot of force behind it. Just one move: *boom!* I smacked him. Not having planned on this, I was wearing a white button-down shirt, so when I hit him—as I grabbed his head and pulled it toward my knee—his blood covered my shirt. That was all that my cousins—who frequented the bar—needed to see: me covered in blood. So they swarmed over, rushing to my aid. Everything just got more violent from there. When the dust settled, everyone was basically fine except for the supposed tough guy. He got his ass kicked *and* he got arrested.

Wow. I can still see Jaime's face, her eyes big and wide at what must have been a world she'd never witnessed. That was always surreal for any of my friends from civilized LA who went down to Tijuana and caught a glimpse of what it was like to be in a place where anarchy ruled. But because of my efforts to stay cool and collected (for the most part), being with me, she seemed to feel safe. When I checked to make sure, Jaime assured me that she knew nothing was going to happen to us down there. Actually, I suspect that seeing that side of me come out might have turned her on.

But there was no amount of toughness that could help me recoup my investment. After more years of asking Tommy to repay the money and hearing him say over and over again, "This month wasn't good," I saw the writing on the wall. There was one month when he brought me four grand, but that was it.

So, rounding down, I lost sixty grand on the worst financial decision of my life. It was a $60,000 party. Finally, I got out.

Sixty thousand dollars is a lot for anyone to lose. Thankfully, I was young enough to bounce back, but as I veered into my midtwenties in a post–A. C. Slater state of mind, I understood a new reality: that being an entertainer is a job in which one day you can be hot and the next you might as well be in the witness protection program for how much people remember you. In other words, bouncing back was never guaranteed.

On a positive note, there is something to be said for making a bad business decision to keep you from ever making another one like it again. To my credit, I didn't give up on being entrepreneurial and I didn't lose my determination not to put all the eggs in one showbiz basket. But when it comes to regrets, if I could go back to the nineties I would not have written off this whole Internet thing as a fad. Just imagine if instead of putting that $65,000 in a bar in TJ, I had boldly invested in stock like Microsoft, Apple, and Google. Just imagine.


When I look back at the roller-coaster ride that was most of my twenties, I recall a few lifetimes lived. Not for a minute would I trade any of the dating experiences I was fortunate enough to enjoy. Whenever I hear anything from *Maxwell's Urban Hang Suite*—my go-to jam—it all comes back. (And if we want to talk sound tracks of those years, I happen to be partial to R. Kelly's

*12 Play*, and, trust me, you can never go wrong with Sade.) Even though I wasn't ready to settle down and stick with one lasting relationship, in those years I learned a lot more about women and about enjoying the friendship that comes along with romance.

The best highs of those years were getting to share successes with the people I loved. For example, whenever I traveled to do personal appearances—which started at age eighteen and lasted well into my twenties—I'd take a friend or one of my cousins along for the fun. I was used to the attention but it was brand-new to my guys. I would trip out on how much fun they had while they would trip out on the whole scene of women throwing themselves at us. My friends and cousins are good-looking, charismatic guys, so they did well for themselves in the flirtation department.

"Whoa, I can't believe this—I *can't believe* this!" they'd rejoice, thanking me as though I had superpowers. They didn't perceive me the way fans did—to them I was just their goofy cousin or good ol' pal, who could now somehow help them score with the ladies.

Sharing what I had with my family was always a priority. Maybe because I was raised with such a strong work ethic, I've always maintained a guarded optimism as far as money is concerned. Clearly, with my bad bar investment, I was a tad too optimistic. But after that blunder, my MO in my twenties was to be guardedly optimistic that I could save and invest wisely enough to be able to weather a fickle entertainment business. For survival, when it came to my post-*SBTB* career, I learned to be cautious. To me, everything could end in a heartbeat. A big change from when I was younger and impressed casting people with my *Que será será* cool. My new mantra soon became: "Hope for the best but expect the worst." Maybe that was me toughening up for the changes in the industry in general, but I adopted the attitude that if my entire career came to a screeching halt, my family and I would still be secure.

My point is that I don't keep much money in the bank. For me, it's better to reinvest it, wisely, or put it to use taking care of my family and friends. Though they never ask me for money, I love being able to take care of them when I can, like putting my sister, Marissa, through college at San Diego State University.

Granted, in my twenties I was only beginning to have a grasp of what this all meant. I never had financial goalposts set in my mind. Money was important to me, sure, but I've never thought about it in those benchmark terms. Mom did have the right idea, though, when she urged me at age eighteen to buy that first little house—which I still own today. Well, it's actually in the process of being torn down so I can build three condos on the site. With the investment in other properties in the Chula area that I made after that, I have come a long way since buying that first house. And now that I'm living in LA, I have a dozen properties here too.

My business instincts have improved since my late teens, for sure, and I don't have to worry about the upkeep as my mom manages all of my properties for me. Also, investing in real estate is fairly practical. People will always need a place to live. Plus, I've watched entrepreneurs like Donald Trump and Arnold Schwarzenegger make their fortunes by buying property, so I've been reasonably confident that real estate investment is making a safe bet. So far so good—even if I'm by no means at the level of The Donald or the former Governor.

But none of this security or sanity came overnight. Career-wise, the post-*SBTB* road turned out to be much rockier than I'd anticipated. The more time I had on my hands without my next acting role after the series ended, the more I questioned my decision not to go to college. It was sometimes a dark place. Besides worrying about how I was going to make money going forward, for the first time in my life I started questioning and doubting my abilities. The questions ate at me. Had I only lucked out as a child actor? Was this what I really wanted to do? Had I "made it" only to see it all fade? Was this as good as it was going to get?

Most of the time, I was my usual upbeat, high-energy self, going strong and doing smaller roles as they came my way. But there were periods when the calls were less frequent and more suited to actors just starting in their careers. Like an athlete, I had to pump myself up with pep talks, telling myself that *of course* I was unique enough and special enough in terms of my talent and passion—that I had something authentic of my own to offer. There weren't many people like me in the industry, as far as I could tell. Not many young Latinos were taking the path I had chosen, no question. And I felt as if I had a certain energy that made me stand out and that I hoped was infectious to others. That I could contribute to any project—and elevate the work in general.

My saving grace during these slow periods was having a great family who loved and supported me. That, and turning over all of that which I couldn't control to my higher power. Family and faith have always served me, in good times and bad, as have those events that seemed to come along and put everything in perspective.

One such event took place during these years when the family became concerned about how seldom we'd seen or heard from my favorite cousin, Louie, who'd grown up right across the street from me. Louie, my good-looking *primo* with the smile that lit up the room whenever he entered it, had moved away from Chula Vista to Minneapolis when he was about nineteen. The strange part was that he had been going to college locally for a short time and then abruptly moved. We were all busy with our own lives, so we didn't think much of his sudden departure when it happened. At first, he appeared to make regular efforts to come back and visit the relatives and the gang from the neighborhood.

On one of his visits, I heard some of the cousins say Louie had been seen in the Hillcrest area of San Diego, a neighborhood that had a large gay community. Some of the relatives began to gossip about how they'd always sensed he was different. But I didn't care— it was none of my business, and I just wanted him to be happy. He never really opened up to me about being gay, and though I regretted not having done more to let him know he could always talk to me, I figured, well, he would have said something if *he* wanted to.

On one of his visits, Louie finally told his brother that he was gay but that it was too difficult to come out of the closet, as a Latino and as a Catholic.

While this conversation went well, and Louie's brother expressed our family's love and support, it didn't get Louie to open up and tell the rest of the family. He insisted he just couldn't. It was so sad. We started seeing him less and less until one day I came into the house and heard the strangest, most mournful sound. My father had just been told that Louie, his brother's son, had taken a huge overdose of pills and had gone to sleep for good.

That was the first and only time I ever saw my father cry. My dad is a real tough guy, and to see him cry just broke my heart. Louie's death put all my so-called worry about my career and whatnot into perspective, reminding me how fragile life really is. Seeing my dad crying so inconsolably made *me* cry. I promised to find a way to honor Louie's memory if the opportunity ever came along to do so. The truth is, I never thought about it this way until now, but I have to believe that the opportunity did come—sooner than I could have guessed.

• • •

"Greg Louganis?" I asked my agent when I was first sent the script for a movie of the week that had been in search of its star.

"Take a look and let me know what you think," my agent suggested, not selling the project one way or the other.

True, I might not have been the obvious choice to play Greg Louganis, the Olympic gold medalist and gay icon, but from the moment I read the script, I sensed that this was the role I'd been waiting for. It could definitely help me shed the skin of my A. C. Slater persona and usher in new possibilities for my career. What's more, I had been a major fan of Greg Louganis since the day I saw him compete in the 1984 Olympics. He also happened to be from San Diego, which enhanced our connection in my view. And when, a short time later, I was offered the role, I was thrilled. From an acting standpoint, at the age of twenty-three, I wanted and needed the challenge and the shot to be seen in a new light—as a serious adult, no longer a kid actor, and nothing like Slater. This was my chance to prove myself and bring the behind-the-scenes story of Greg Louganis to an even larger worldwide audience.

The movie was based on Greg's bestselling memoir, *Breaking the Surface*, and there was great pressure both to do the book justice and to accurately depict what he went through in his career, especially at the time of the Olympics. Not just that, but as I was portraying someone who was still alive, that meant he and his friends would be watching closely to see whether I had captured his essence as a young man and champion.

Greg, the most critical judge, was right there on set with us to score my performance! I doubt that I could have been any more intimidated. Much to my relief and gratitude, Greg was supportive and an all-around awesome guy from beginning to end. And he was pleased with my portrayal, which was what mattered most to me.

The role was physical, which I loved, but it involved a crash course in high diving. I've never been afraid of heights and I've always loved swimming, but diving was something else. Diving and what they call "air awareness" were necessary for me to master if I was going to be good at this role and convince people, for two-plus hours, that I was an Olympic diver. Guess what. Out of all the activities Mom put on my childhood roster, diving was not one of them. In fact, I had never dived before and I had to learn how to dive reasonably well in time for the first day of principle photography. As in, right away. But hey, that's how the business rolls. Directors usually don't give you a year to learn a skill when you're the lead in a film; you're given perhaps a few months and then they yell, "Action!"

How did I get up to speed? Pun intended, I dove right in. Literally. I went to the nearest pool with a regulation high diving board—ten meters or thirty feet—and started trying the various jumps and dives I'd seen done by amateurs and pros alike. In one of my first practice sessions, I jumped off the high dive and became so disoriented that I landed on my back—*smack!*—and had the wind knocked out of me. The feeling of hitting the water with that force, from that height and at that velocity, was as if I had hit the ground. After that, I was sufficiently humbled and scared enough to not try to man up and do it on my own. In fact, I was able to train with the USC diving team and then even Louganis helped me a little bit, just so I could get comfortable on the board.

The movie pushed me out of my comfort zone in other ways too. Besides the diving, the script called for me to kiss a guy. For a straight man, kissing another guy, even if you're an actor and you're just playing a part, is uncomfortable at best. But if that was in the job description, no complaints from me. However, I thought that before going on set and starting to film, it might be a good idea to prepare my dad for what he would see when the movie aired.

"Dad," I began, when I sat him down over a weekend visit home, "about this movie, you know besides the diving, it's also Greg's personal story, right?" He hadn't read the script, so he shrugged and waited for me to go on.

I hesitated, searching for the right words. My dad was always supportive and he truly never had a homophobic bone in his body. But I'm still his son and, old-school macho guy that Dad is, I didn't want him to freak out later on and think that I'd purposely kept something from him. It was important for me to let him know that I didn't have any issue with it because this was true to the real-life person I was going to be portraying and, as an actor, I had to be true to that, no matter how awkward I'd feel. In trying to be sensitive, I was hoping too that if I prepared my dad, he would also get the word out to the rest of my family and our friends. This was, after all, a less open-minded time than today. Audiences were more judgmental and there weren't public forums in support of gay marriage or shows on television like *Glee* that openly portrayed gay relationships. In fact, this movie was taking chances with subject matter seldom touched on—issues not only related to sexuality but also about bullying and family dysfunction.

"So," I finally explained, sort of, "there may be a surprise or two, you know . . ." With his look of confusion, I went on to say that there was going to be a scene between me and the actor portraying Greg's boyfriend.

"Well, what the hell are you going to be doing?" my dad barked.

"I don't really know."

"Fine," he said, thinking about it. "Just don't fall in love with the guy!" Then he laughed. And that was that.

At the time, I didn't really know everything the director was planning to shoot or how he would shoot it. Dad was cool with whatever I had to do to play this role and so too were my mom and the rest of the family.

So, with those discussions behind me, the day came at last to shoot the scene that would require me to kiss the actor playing Greg's partner, Tom. I understood that this was supposed to be a loving moment and was ready to let the director tell us what his vision was and let us just go for it with the camera rolling. Kind of like diving off the high dive. Only, instead of taking the plunge on set, the actor playing Tom wanted to rehearse ahead of time.

"Rehearse?" I asked, not without trepidation. But then, thinking about it, I thought we might as well get it out of the way. If we rehearsed, we would look professional and comfortable. "Yeah," I agreed. "You're right. Let's rehearse."

So we kissed. The best I can say is that it was weird. The worst part, as I recall, was that I thought I felt tongue. Yikes. After rehearsal I kept hoping not to have to do it for the camera. But it was what it was—part of the job description.

We get to the set the next day and—surprise!—the director cuts the scene. Talk about a bittersweet moment. On the one hand, I was relieved not to kiss on camera, and on the other hand, I now realized I had kissed my fellow actor in a rehearsal for absolutely no reason. I felt like Lucy in the Charlie Brown cartoon when Snoopy licks her face and the caption reads, "Yuck."

I laughed so hard that I had kissed a dude for nothing. The other actor may have been a bit disappointed. He told me I was a good kisser.

Other than that twist in the real-life plot, *Breaking the Surface* was a blessing at that time in my life and career. It certainly helped open doors to career opportunities that would have remained closed. Perhaps not as many as every actor would love all the time, but that's showbiz—you have to fight not to be pigeonholed into a Hollywood "type." Just as important is how tackling the role allowed me to grow up, open my mind to new possibilities as a performer, and move past the mind-set of A. C. Slater.

One of my prouder moments came in 1998 when I was nominated for an ALMA Award for *Breaking the Surface*. I wasn't overly disappointed that I didn't win, except I would have liked to have been able to hold up the award and say to my cousin Louie, "*Primo*, this one's for you." Or acknowledge him in some way. But truly I was honored to be there. These awards, sponsored by the National Council of La Raza, were always a reminder of the need for more representation of Latinos and Latino artists in the entertainment field. Of course, as a Mexican kid who grew up in the barrio, that had long been an issue for me. But on that occasion, when I had the chance to rub shoulders with fellow nominees in different categories, I realized for the first time that it was time for me to step up and do more to promote opportunities for all of us within our diverse Hispanic community. At the time, I wasn't sure how to go about taking on a cause like that. What I was sure about was that striving to be successful would only help—in whatever form that success was to take.

What was to stop me? Well, frankly, me. Yep, as an adult, I was still the same high-energy kid that my mom tried to keep out of trouble by making me take dance classes and wrestling and karate. Clearly, something that required an intense level of discipline and training, something new that I could learn to master, was exactly what I needed for focus and balance.

And you know what they say: seek and ye shall find. They also say that when the student is ready, the teacher appears.

Both held true for me.

• • •

The sign on the door read "Wild Card Boxing Club" and it was owned by Freddie Roach, one of the most famous trainers of all time. The gym sits right in the middle of a seedy section of Hollywood on top of a Chinese Laundromat and next to a well-attended meeting place for Alcoholics Anonymous.

In mid-2001, I was in my late twenties and had lived in Hollywood for about a decade, so I must have driven by the Wild Card Boxing Club numerous times. That summer I had just started working on developing a TV talk show that was slated to be like *Oprah* but for men, and I was spending a lot of time at the Sunset Gower Studios over on that side of town.

There was nothing glamorous about this gym. Outside on the street, no urban renewal plan had come in yet to improve the neighborhood for tourists or locals. You can picture it: trash everywhere, stray cats, homeless people strolling around. It was just the hood, the sort of place you'd find most boxing gyms. But for quite a while there was something about the sign on the door and the gym's reputation that had made me want to go check it out. Finally, after a meeting at the studio one evening, I stopped making excuses and walked over, pushing past the sign on the door and into another world.

Boxing! Why hadn't I thought of it sooner? Ever since high school, when I wrestled competitively for the last time, I had needed a physical outlet as a way to release pent-up aggression. Boxing was much more suited to my enjoyment of the more aggressive combat-type sports, specifically one-on-one competition. Wrestling and boxing are similar in many ways in that they have a simplistic, primal, and pure essence at their root. Man on man. One on one. There are no team members and no one to rely on. If you lose a fight, it's because of you. When you win the fight, you get all the glory. While there are boxing matches in which I think the judges must be blind, in general it's the best man who wins the battle.

As a fan of professional boxing since I was a kid, I grew up with aficionados of the sport all around. My grandfather Tata Trasvina, my mom's dad, boxed back in Mexico in his youth, so it was in my blood all along. Plus, I knew about the similarities between wrestling and boxing. In watching boxers over the years, I recognized the need for a boxer to have self-knowledge. Training and sparring give you the chance to get to know yourself and to gauge what you are made of as you step in a ring. You learn to push yourself past your own limits and see yourself under the direst circumstances, as in a fight. Whether it's wrestling or boxing, it's definitely a fight. There are skills, technique, fundamentals, and rules, but it's a fight. In structured combat like wrestling and boxing, we get a chance to unleash that part of our human nature as men that has a primitive desire to beat out the other man—to fight.

As I cruised into the gym the first time, all of that intensity was on display. The vibe was gritty and tough, with the same cool-looking boxing gym setup you'd see in the *Rocky* films. But the difference here was a) this was the real deal, and b) I could look around and see world champions training next to ex-cons, ex-cons training next to businessmen. Everyone was so compatible with one another and the energy was electric.

When I spotted Freddie, trainer of everyone from Mike Tyson to Oscar De La Hoya, he was quietly watching a young boxer hitting one of the big bags. The inimitable Freddie Roach, raised in the Boston area, was about forty at the time, and with his blond hair, slightly graying and cut short, and a pair of nondescript glasses, he almost looked like an absentminded college professor.

Maybe that's why one of his nicknames was "The Choir Boy." But looks can be deceiving. Freddie's other nickname was La Cucaracha—the Cockroach, who is indestructible—because he was just that tough. Freddie had been trained by the legendary Eddie Futch—who coached such boxers as Joe Frazier and Ken Norton—and Master Roach drew from Futch's approach to the ring. What they said about Freddie is that he trained boxers to utilize mental strategy in the ring, a more quiet but lethal mind-set to disarm opponents. Freddie used to say that he couldn't change a fighter but he could take what they had naturally and work to improve it.

There was no hesitation on my part. I walked across the room, greeted Freddie, and asked, "Hey, can I just drop in and start working out?"

Freddie Roach shrugged and said, "Yeah. Just come in."

It was five dollars a day or fifty dollars a month. It started out as just a thing where I would go into the gym, hit the bag, and train like a boxer. I had never really boxed or had any boxing training. What I knew was from wrestling, and—probably from dance—I had good balance. I also seemed to know how to be relaxed in the ring, which is tough to do when the guy across from you is looking to punch your lights out. Boxing came naturally or I just took to it. You could say I fell in love with it right away—love at first punch.

I loved everything about it: I loved the camaraderie in the gym, I loved the colorful characters in the sport, and I loved, most of all, the sparring. No surprise there. Sparring at the training level is where you get in that ring and you fight without having to go multiple rounds. Still, you box a live human being, not an inanimate bag that can't punch back. Oh, but that was just a warm-up for me. I was hooked. Given how well I'd taken to sparring, I decided, why not go one step farther and put myself in harm's way?

Eventually, that led to the decision to participate in some amateur sorts of bouts. Freddie Roach has these things he calls "smokers," which are three-round sanctioned fights. He matches you up—according to your ability and your weight—against another opponent who works out at the gym. You go in there and you fight for three three-minute rounds of fury. Boxers in smokers wear protective headgear to prevent getting cuts on their face. But you can still very easily get knocked out. You can still get a concussion. You can still get the crap beat out of you.

I had followed the basic three steps, not rushing the process too much: 1) I started my training. 2) It wasn't long before I wanted to spar. 3) I began testing my skills by participating in the smokers. Regardless of how much you train, how tough you think you are, or how ready you might be to get in the ring, nothing really prepares you for the moment of truth when you lift up that rope and climb inside for the first time.

In an almost out-of-body state, I felt my palms sweating under the gloves and protective wraps. My heart sounded and felt as if it was going to pound right out of my chest and the air rushed frenetically in and out of my nose like no normal breathing I'd ever known. I was going to do this. I was really going to fight someone.

The bell rang and we met in the middle of the ring and tapped gloves. We began, as many fighters do, dancing around, throwing jabs and feints to see what the other guy's style was. Then—*pop*—I hit him with a right and he returned with a shot to my ribs. It was on. My adrenaline spiked, pumping on all cylinders, and I attacked with everything I had. At the same time, he came at me hard, with hits to my head from right and left. Dizzy, I shook off those blows and kept coming. In my brain, the goal was to prove to myself and to my opponent that I was dedicated and willing to look bad before I could get good. I won the fight that day but I was humbled. I fell even more deeply in love and tied a lasting knot with my new passion: boxing.

Seeking some degree of moderation, I tried not to overdo it, but in the years that followed I went on to fight in a total of six smokers and would remain undefeated. Once I was even awarded "Fighter of the Night" for one of my more dramatic fights. My record includes knocking out four of the six guys I'd been set up to fight. One time, however, I was the one who got dropped hard. Up until that point I had never gotten knocked down to the mat. But I've never gone down since. One guy showed up as a last-minute opponent. He was a very tough guy—an MMA fighter—and just the man to set me straight. Not only was he an MMA fighter, but he also fought southpaw. Adding insult to my soon-to-be injury was the fact that he was also a big guy and heavier than me by a good fifteen pounds.

My original opponent canceled out, and Freddie said, "Look, this guy's a tough guy, a real—you know, he's a real fighter. Are you sure you want to do this? He can fight. Do you want to fight him?"

Already warmed up and raring to go, I eyed this big, ripped guy on the other side of the ring, wondering if I could handle him. But I had trained really hard and couldn't chicken out. "Yeah, let's do it," I told Freddie. He gave a look, squinting behind his glasses, as if I wasn't too convincing. "Yeah, man," I persisted. "I want to fight. I want to push myself."

So we got in the ring and toed off, and it wasn't long before he caught me with a hard shot to the head. I had hurt him with a body shot in the first round, but here in the second round he caught me good with that big left hook. Remember, he was fighting southpaw and I wasn't used to a left-hander. So when he caught me with that left hook, oooh, I went down. I don't even remember. Somehow, I got back up and shook it off. Because I'm in pretty good shape, I can usually take a shot too. But he was strong. At the bell, I was still out of it and they poured some water on my head, enough so that I woke up and regained my bearings. After the explosive hook he landed on my head, I fought a little bit more cautiously in the third round. With only a minute or so left in the round, I sensed that he was tired and knew that if I was going to win this I had to step it up. That's mental strategy, looking for your opponent's weaknesses and exploiting them. In a flash, I saw my opening and threw the hardest punch I could muster. I dropped him. That was the Fight of the Night. How could I not be hooked on boxing for good?

When I fight in the smokers, I always get my opponent's best efforts. They may not say it or show it, but the last thing someone wants to do is to get their ass kicked by some Hollywood pretty-boy kid. But if you asked Freddie Roach, he'd tell you that I've earned the respect of everyone in the gym. Even though I've probably had more knockouts than anyone else who has fought in the smokers, new opponents who are thinking of fighting me have been known to say, "Ah, you know, that pretty boy with his little dimples, man, he can't fight—he's just all show." Or they assume that even if I can fight and have some skills, that I'm not tough enough. So they test me.

Boxing is an equalizer when it comes to toughness. The guys who are really tough don't have to try to prove anything. The guys who think they're tough and try to prove I'm not—well, that fires me up in the ring and they end up getting a little bit hurt. The Wild Card Boxing Club gave me a space to change a lot of people's misconceptions about me. In gaining the respect of the boxers who train there, I was able to become not some Hollywoody type, but just one of the guys at the gym.

Questions come at me all the time: "Well, why do you do it, man? You make your living with your face. And you're putting yourself at risk and your career in jeopardy, and all these people who depend on you." Even my close friends caution me, "Lopez, you and people who need you are going to be in a world of hurt if you get a serious head injury or your nose ends up on the wrong side of your face."

Others want to know why I don't play a mellower sport. Basketball, golf, and so on. Those are fine, and fun too; some of the entertainment sports leagues are collegial and festive. But they are nowhere near as exhilarating as fighting. Back in my late twenties, I learned this truth about me: I want to, I have to, and I need to fight.

It's the way I'm wired—could be the underdog in me, the fighter that's part of who I am. When I'm old and my body is broken down, then maybe I'll take up golf—with no disrespect to anyone who loves being on the green as much as I love being in the ring. For now, I'm still too energetic and need the challenge. Maybe if golf were a contact sport and you got to battle each other with the clubs. Tennis isn't for me either—again, no offense to you tennis lovers. Trust me, I'm not that good at tennis. I didn't grow up in Beverly Hills; I'm not a country club kid. Tennis might be too polite for me.

Boxing keeps me young, sharp, fresh, and focused. Come to think of it, I'm going to be boxing for the rest of my life if I can. In fact, I've sparred with guys in their sixties, so I believe there's hope. Let me add that it takes a certain type of individual to step into a boxing ring. Maybe you have to be a little bit crazy—but *I'm* a little bit crazy, so it fits. Also, for me, from a practical standpoint, boxing travels well—which is part of my daily grind. If I want to spar or work out while I'm on the road, it's fairly easy to find a boxing gym or at least a facility that has a punching bag. It's easier to carry some gloves, shorts, wraps, and sneakers than it is a set of golf clubs.

Not too long ago, I was given an opportunity to start calling fights for HBO Boxing. My gigs as a boxing announcer haven't taken over my career, but it's fun and I get to watch my heroes fight from a vantage point that is even better than ringside seats. I'm literally on the ring apron. I get to call these fights and give my honest opinion of the action at hand. I've called fights for Top Rank, Golden Boy, on HBO Boxing, and on Showtime Boxing. I have come to know the boxing community well, including all the promoters and all the miscellaneous people in the sport. Boxing is part of my multifaceted career in hosting that I had only begun to conceive back in mid-2001 when this all started. Boxing also fed my mantra that you may have heard me repeat elsewhere: "I work out more for sanity than for vanity." Yes, boxing, as crazy as this may sound, keeps me sane. It's a release from all the pent-up stress most of us have in our work and daily dramas and day-to-day aggravations. You can't punch the face of the person who just cut you off in traffic, or the bad customer service representative, or the meter maid who just wrote you a huge ticket, but you can punch a sparring partner or a punching bag.

Suffice it to say, life after A. C. Slater went on, and I tried to savor the ups and downs of all that I was fortunate enough to experience and learn. But new questions began to eat at me about what the future was going to bring. At the same time, I could feel big changes in the wind. But how they would happen and where they would take me, I had no idea. All I could do was stay focused and watch out for those big left hooks.

# CHAPTER 6

# TURNING POINTS

It began as a sort of flirtation in the late 1990s, then turned into a fling that would deepen into a solid relationship over the next four or five years. At a certain point, I realized we just fit together. However, with other interests and opportunities that came along, I always held back from that exclusive commitment I really did want to make—but somehow couldn't.

Oh, wait. You don't think I'm talking about my love life, do you? Nope, not at all, even though I could have been. I'm talking about the unexpected passion I found in my late twenties for . . . hosting! That's right, my path to becoming a host in the wide, wide wonderful world of entertainment was a lot like dating at first. In fact, earlier in my career, back when I was eighteen and on *Saved by the Bell*, I had started to dabble in off-season hosting jobs—and had a ball doing them.

The suggestion first came from an executive at NBC, *SBTB*'s network. The late Linda Mancuso (may she rest in peace after losing her battle to cancer in recent years) gave me that first shot and I would be eternally grateful to her for it. When she called me in for a meeting, Linda was complimentary, saying, "I love your personality, Mario, and I think you'd be a terrific host for a project that we have in the works."

The project was a reality show based on the premise of making kids' dreams come true. The show was to be called *Name Your Adventure* and would air on Saturday mornings just like our series. When she asked if I'd be interested in hosting it, I was intrigued enough to take the job. Of course, my focus overall was my acting career. But this was an opportunity to play myself—not A. C. Slater—and a chance to explore a side job to acting that seemed made to order.

*Name Your Adventure* was positioned to be educational yet still entertainment—what's sometimes called "edutainment." The challenge was to find new ways to casually introduce the educational elements. As a result, I learned to do research on my own to come up with all those fun facts, a skill that would serve me well in time to come. Our format included showing up at the home of that episode's lucky teen and, along with our guides and professional experts, provide the tools for that kid to go off on the adventure of his or her dreams. We climbed mountains, swam with sharks, and went on a cattle drive in Montana. Probably the highlight of the three seasons we shot was fulfilling the dream of one teen to interview the president of the United States—President Bill Clinton. Also right up my alley were the different action sports I had a chance to play alongside our guest athletes. That was quite possibly my favorite gig ever.

*Name Your Adventure* was that first exposure that made me think hosting, which is not acting per se, could still open up other avenues for me as a performer. Other little hosting-type jobs continued from there in connection to the *Saved by the Bell* franchise and I found that hosting suited the part of me that preferred to stay humble. What other role lets you be starstruck on purpose? For example, there was the time early on in the midnineties when NBC had me on hand for special events connected to the NBA's All-Star basketball game in Phoenix, Arizona—a weekend-long summit of top athletes and celebrities who show up as much for the parties and charity functions as they do for the slam-dunk contest and the game itself. During this particular weekend, I was blown away when I found myself hanging out with Will Smith. The Will Smith, then of NBC's *Fresh Prince of Bel-Air* fame. Maybe you've heard of it?

Will was very cool and gracious. Of course, his stellar career would only continue to escalate from this time on, but I was already a big fan. In fact, I had followed him since his hip-hop days as the second half of DJ Jazzy Jeff & the Fresh Prince and loved two of their rap songs, "Parents Just Don't Understand" and "Summertime." Will had his crew of boys from Philly with him, but they were in no way "cliquey" like certain celebs can be with their entourages. Over the years after that weekend, whenever Will and I would run into each other, his face would light up, as would mine.

After hosting gigs like the NBA All-Star weekend, I did begin to think, You know, I could see myself doing more of this. There were moments during other, smaller hosting jobs when I would look around and have to pinch myself. I would actually turn to friends of mine who'd come along for the ride and say, "Oh my God, can you believe they pay me to do this?"

My buddy Juancho came with me to the 1994 NBA All-Star weekend in Minneapolis, and while I was working, word arrived that I had been invited to Prince's house for a party.

If you have never heard of Prince's legendary parties, let me just say that the invitation was exclusive—that is, just for me. Nobody walks through the door without waiting in line and being thoroughly vetted.

"Don't worry, Juancho," I promised my friend. "You're with me. We'll both get in."

Just watching the people waiting in line was like a Who's Who

of 1990s Famous Names. Unbelievable. They made Magic Johnson wait in line. When we all finally got in, it was like walking into
a dream—like a big nightclub. There were athletes and beautiful
models, faces from the news, and, of course, stars from music,
movies, and TV.

"What do you think, Juancho?" I asked. But he was literally
too dumbstruck to respond.

"You know," I said under my breath, "I can't believe we are
inside Prince's house. What the hell are we doing at his house with
all these famous people? Is this amazing or what?"

"Amazing," he finally said.

It's true, by the way: Prince does party like it's 1999! It was
surreal. The party kept rocking and at two in the morning Prince
decided to do a concert. What an incredibly intimate setting in
which to watch him perform—for three full hours. Imagine just
partying with all your new friends and hearing all your favorite
Prince songs in, basically, his living room! And watching the sun
come up as you stumble home. Amazing.

The best way to get a sense of how surreal that night was is to
watch Dave Chappelle's hilarious impression of Prince in a sketch
for his show. In it, Prince serves Charlie Murphy (Eddie Murphy's
brother) grapes and then challenges him to a basketball duel they
call the Blouses Versus the Skins. Juancho and I laughed so hard
years later when we saw it on *Chappelle's Show*. You can check it
out on YouTube to see what it was like to party with Prince—I
promise you'll laugh out loud.

After all these experiences, not surprisingly, I loved hosting.
But once I graduated from *Saved by the Bell* and moved into my
twenties—while seeking out strong acting roles in projects like
*Breaking the Surface*—I still couldn't see building a meaningful

Mom's cowboy action figure.

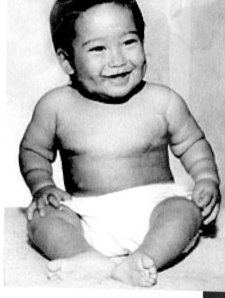

There are those fat rolls I mentioned.

Chubby cheeks and a slick hairdo.

Early signs of mullet love.

Modeling in Chula Vista.

My mom didn't know I was too young for Vegas.

Me and my sister, Marissa; we haven't changed a bit.

MARIO LOPEZ
"KIDS, INC."

REPRESENTED BY
INTERNATIONAL ARTISTS

My first head shot.

Putting on the Ritz.

On my way to the
"gun show."

So much time spent on
the wrestling mats.

Looking good in a promo shot for
*Saved by the Bell.* NBC/Getty Images

With my friend Elizabeth Berkley during the
filming for a spin-off movie, *Saved by the Bell:*
*Hawaiian Style.* NBC/Getty Images

Posing with Mark-Paul
Gosselaar and Dustin
Diamond in the early
days of *Saved by the Bell.*
NBC/Getty Images

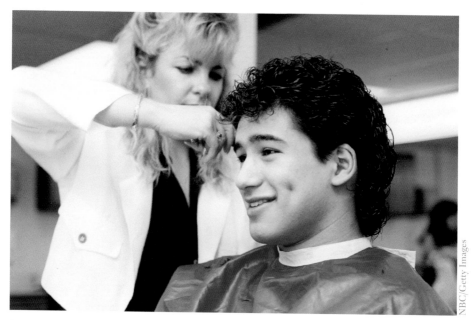

NBC/Getty Images

It was a lot of work keeping up the mullet, and I spent a lot of time in the hair and makeup.

Aww, Tiffani!

My dad made some sort of dirty comment.

Mom and I traveling in style.

Winning smiles from me and Karina Smirnoff on *Dancing with the Stars.*

With Eva Longoria, showing them how it's done at the 2007 ALMA Awards.

Performing on a Broadway stage during my run in *A Chorus Line*.

Cohosting
*The View*
in 2014.

Eva Longoria dropping by to say
hi at my radio show.

With the judges of *The X Factor*:
Demi Lovato, Paulina Rubio, Kelly
Rowland, and Simon Cowell.

Going over who's still in the
competition on *The X Factor*.

*Top:* With George Lopez when the *Extra* set was at Universal Studios Hollywood.

*Left:* With my dad while shooting the cover of *Fitness RX* magazine.

*Bottom left:* One the best fighters of all time, Manny Pacquiao.

*Bottom right:* Now, here's a guy who knows branding: Donald Trump.

Per Bernal

And the Oscar goes to…

Sticking with the dress code at the Emmy Awards.

Moët toast at the Golden Globes.

Jennifer looks amazing at the Grammy Awards. Not sure if I'm loving my suit.

*Top left:* Red-carpet night with the Hollywood icon Julia Roberts.

*Top right:* You have to love DeGeneres. I've been on more than any other guest to date! Thanks, Ellen!

*Left:* Cohosting with Kelly Ripa.

*Bottom left:* Boxing god and good friend Oscar De La Hoya.

*Bottom right:* At a ceremony for my favorite organization, Boys & Girls Club of America.

Celebrating our Emmy Award for Outstanding Entertainment News Program with *Extra*'s exec producer Lisa Gregorisch-Dempsey.

The Emmy Award made an appearance on *Extra*.

On the beach in Mexico after my proposal to Courtney.

The perfect wedding in Mexico. Gia helped with the rose petals.

Mr. and Mrs. Lopez.

Glamorous
life as a dad.

My amazing mother.

Gia and Dominic on Easter.

Our dog, Julio, looking for a treat.

Three generations of Lopez men.

Marissa's family and mine on vacation: what we do best.

career as a host. That is, until I encountered a series of turning points that would slowly but surely make me think twice.

"How tall are you?" my agent asked me over the phone one day back in 1999.

That was a strange question. At the age of twenty-six, I had been the same height for a while and I was pretty sure my agent knew the answer: "Five foot eleven."

The reason for the cryptic question? There was a role in a new Chuck Norris TV series, *Sons of Thunder*, which was supposed to be a spin-off of *Walker, Texas Ranger*. It was perfect for me. Because I would be testing opposite Chuck Norris, the producers had to ask how tall I was. "Say you're shorter," I was advised.

Why? Well, apparently, Norris didn't like anybody to be taller than him.

The producers advised: wear flats to look even shorter.

The test went really well and I thought I'd nailed the role of a tough Dallas cop. But it turned out I was still a little too tall. So I didn't get the part. Seems that Chuck Norris can be a badass as long as he's taller than you.

Still, I just wanted to work. I didn't have the luxury of mapping out a plan, and saying, "I want to work with Steven Spielberg, Francis Ford Coppola, or only the top-name directors." My only goal was to be consistently working. Given the work ethic that was cultivated in me throughout my childhood—essentially a hustler's mentality—I wasn't going to look down my nose at any opportunity that came my way. But even if my priorities were sometimes screwed up, I wanted to be good at what I did, so it was important to work on projects that would challenge me and take me to a higher level.

Finding just *any* kind of work wasn't a problem. But getting jobs that allowed me to grow as an artist—that was a different story.

Sometimes I missed out on getting a coveted role merely because of how I look. I may have auditioned for something and they were open to seeing me, but it was more curiosity on their part. In that case, I could usually tell I wasn't going to get it. For example, if I'm auditioning to play the son in the family, and the mom and the dad are already cast, and they look like the Wonder Bread parents from *Family Ties*, I'm not going to look like their son no matter how much I impress them in the reading.

The reality check for me—true for many of us in the business—is that when you go to the audition, you can be the best actor in the room but that's no guarantee you'll get the part. You can blow them away and surpass every other contender, but sometimes it doesn't matter. Because maybe you're a little too old, a little too tall, or too short. You're not Caucasian enough; you don't look like you're related to the existing cast. Whatever the case may be, you're not going to get the part if you don't fit all those variables and intangibles. You rarely find out exactly why. So many factors come into play and so many elements are outside your control. Not to mention the politics involved—even the nepotism involved (in case the producer has a nephew that's up for your role). A hundred and one factors can snub you and your chance of getting that job.

"You're only as good as your last job" is a cliché that's one hundred percent true. And when your last job is something as specific as Greg Louganis in a TV movie or something as crystallized in public memory as A. C. Slater, that means it becomes even more difficult to get good work—because casting directors and producers can't see you as someone else.

So what do you do? In my case, I arrived at a turning point and began to rethink how I saw hosting in general. In mid-2001, as the new millennium began, I was almost twenty-eight. Cable and network TV were booming with greater than ever opportunities for great hosts to make their mark. The entrepreneur in me said, "Why not?" and the creative soul in me realized that being a host would challenge me to grow and learn. And just as I was coming to that conclusion, the universe tapped me on the shoulder to let me know that I was headed in the right direction.

Actually, the tap on the shoulder was real. It came, once again, at a moment when I was ready—no, *hungry*—to learn. That nudge forward was from the Jedi Master of hosting, Dick Clark, who had so very much to teach me.

D ick Clark not only ascended the show business ladder to make his mark as the host of *American Bandstand*—which aired for thirty years, starting in 1957—but in my opinion he helped build the ladder toward stardom for entertainers of every type. There was probably no aspect of entertainment media that Dick Clark didn't touch—radio, TV, game shows, music, live events, talk shows, comedy, providing a platform for film stars, you name it. He was everywhere and he was beloved for who he was and how he made you, the viewer, feel included in whatever rocking party he was hosting. At this writing, he hasn't been gone long, but I miss him every day and wonder sometimes whether New Year's Eve will ever be the same without him behind the mic at Times Square.

Working with Dick Clark was the single most influential and

pivotal experience of my life. Beyond what I learned as a host, Dick's guidance reshaped everything I'd thought about and had planned for my future. By example, he encouraged me to focus more on being a personality and a brand, rather than only as an actor-performer. For us creative folks, it's not easy to make this leap, but getting to study the architecture of Dick Clark Productions got me thinking of myself, Mario Lopez, as a business.

As one of the cohosts for this new show called *The Other Half*—billed as the male version of *The View*—I had a seat right next to Dick Clark, who took the older, wiser, Barbara Walters point of view. I bounced off him easily as the young bachelor with fresh takes on various concerns.

Danny Bonaduce, from *The Partridge Family*, was on the show as well, though he seemed mostly worried about being funny and wasn't really paying attention to anything else. Rounding out our cast was Dr. Jan Adams, a plastic surgeon, who, most unfortunately, was later linked to surgeries that led to Kanye West's mom's death. But no such scandals or tragedies arose for him during the airing of the show.

When filming the first couple of episodes, I realized that I was quarterbacking the show, with the task of taking us from segment to segment, making the transitions, trying to keep us afloat and focused. Dick Clark appreciated that. Even though he wasn't officially producing the show, when Dick was involved with anything, he would bring his unparalleled expertise into play.

Our group on air got along well. I was perhaps more traditional than the rest of the cast and I think Dick identified with that. This was around the same time that I started to build a little more spiritual muscle. My views were changing, as a man, and besides becoming somewhat more conservative than I had been in my wilder younger days, I wanted to be conscious of how my stances could be viewed. Did that mean I was out of the woods in terms of making foolish mistakes in my personal life? Nope. But I was beginning to mature.

On an ominous note, *The Other Half* premiered on September 10, 2001, the day before we all woke up to the news of the terrorist attacks that changed the world forever. In fact, some of us on the show had already arrived at the studio by four a.m. Pacific time to get ready to go on air, so we were there to watch in horror as the reports arrived in real time. After that day, the light banter on the show became more serious for a while. We reflected the mood of the country, I think, and had enough of a viewership to last for three seasons, but no more.

During this time, Dick not only took me under his wing, but the two of us became friends. On several occasions I was a guest at his home, in addition to going out to dinner and to social events with him. A great storyteller, he had many showbiz tales to share and a virtual museum of Hollywood memorabilia in his house. Like the bathroom door that for some reason Michael Jackson had signed and given him, or the framed pieces of clothing and albums and letters from the Beatles, or the gifts from Elvis. Dick said Elvis was the nicest guy—the type of rich guy who wouldn't hesitate to buy you a Cadillac—but that "he wasn't the sharpest tool in the shed."

We talked about investment and how Dick had diversified his interests over the years. Apparently, he owned all the Krispy Kreme donut shops in the UK, as well as an island somewhere and about half of Malibu, California.

Wow.

As a mentor, Dick was direct and the greatest salesman for whatever he believed in. "Mario," he told me early in our relationship, "when you're a host and you've got a good personality and people like you, all you've got to be is likable and relatable, and yourself. Which is hard for some people. But it's easy for you. You'll have much more longevity in this business. Actors come and go, and they're at the whim and detriment of a writer and a director. But if you start looking at yourself as a brand, and focusing on creating opportunities for yourself, and producing, then you can be in here for the long haul."

He was persuasive. "All right," I agreed. "I like that. I'll become the Latino Dick Clark." I said it jokingly, of course. But I meant it too. What I really wanted was to be the all-American host with a little extra spice.

However, before I wedded myself to just being a host, my road to that altar was about to take some more complicated turns.


P ress rewind.

A few years before I made up my mind to move forward full force with hosting, the direction of my personal life had also shifted as the result of one of those earlier hosting gigs. The year was 1998 and I'd been hired to host the Miss Teen USA pageant. 'N Sync with Justin Timberlake played the show that year, which also happened to be their first TV appearance. The sideline reporters for the pageant were Ali Landry and Julie Moran, who worked at *Entertainment Tonight* at the time. When I saw Ali, I immediately recognized her as the girl from a Doritos commercial that had aired during the Super Bowl that year.

Wearing a tank top with a long skirt, she dashed by me walking her dog, Cosmo, a shih tzu. She was a head-turner for sure, but also looked sweet and fresh off the farm. And yep, she was hot. Ali stopped, looked me over in my preshow attire of black Adidas sweatpants and sneakers and a black T-shirt. I looked back at her and smiled.

The timing was not ideal for getting involved with anyone new. At that point, I was very committed to having what I considered to be a noncommittal "good time" in the dating world. There was another issue, as I found out during the flirtatious conversations we had over the weekend: she had a boyfriend—an NFL quarterback or something along those lines.

But we definitely had a spark, so that didn't stop me from telling her, after a couple of cocktails, that we were meant for each other. After the pageant ended and the weekend was nearly done, the producers set up an after-party to which the entire production crew showed up. Feeling something fateful about the moment, I pulled Ali aside and said, "I'm going to marry you, just so you know."

"I have a boyfriend," she reminded me.

I brushed it off. "That's all right. I'm not jealous, and besides, he's not my issue." And then I walked up to her mom, who was with her that weekend, and told her the same thing: that I was going to marry Ali.

What was I thinking? She was this very sweet girl and suddenly the world stopped and she was *it*. But I knew nothing about her, a fact that would soon become a major point of contention.

Some time passed before I was able to convince her to go out to dinner. The timing hadn't improved much. But I was in pursuit, not giving up; Ali was still not available, still in a relationship, even though it sounded rocky. At our first date, I was my unabashed self, unafraid to say that I wanted us to be an "us." Ali seemed interested but restrained—which was just the kind of girl-next-door thing I liked. We casually hung out and kissed for the first time that weekend, and then we started dating shortly afterward.

Press fast-forward now. We're all caught up. So Ali and I dated for six years. That broke all records for me. I thought this was *the* girl. If I wrote down the criteria of what I wanted in a wife and a mother—back then—she seemed to be it. She was a model, so she always had good style—she knew how to dress. And she was Catholic, very driven, ambitious, hardworking—but also charming and innocent at the same time.

I could have been looking at a lot of criteria that were more on the surface than not. But that was my bad. Except a short time later I felt that she seemed to be changing. Like many girls who move here from small towns, Hollywood appeared to be taking its toll on her. Deep down I questioned whether she was the same sweet Southern belle that I'd fallen for. The changes were subtle, but her interests sounded more materialistic and she seemed more preoccupied with image rather than substance, things I didn't care about. Our conversations became less based on common interests and more about her pressuring me to be a *certain way*, dress a certain way, act a certain way.

We all change in Hollywood, especially if we're trying to make it in the industry; it was just a matter of whether we were changing in the same ways. That wasn't her fault, but it confused me.

We had broken up a couple of times over the six years of dating, but I wasn't ready to break up with her forever. We always got back together, every time. When we finally got back together after the last breakup, that's when she gave the ultimatum. Either we would move forward—get married—or she was going to leave me.

Press pause. What to do? Wasn't this a sign that I needed to grow up and get serious with my life—and this was my chance? Or was I confusing the thought that my resistance was just cold feet with legitimately not being ready? Every man should grow up and evolve, but the realistic pace of that evolution is a crucial point. I didn't know the difference between trusting my instincts and questioning my fears. My instincts screamed that I didn't need to rush while my more critical voice barked that it was a manly choice to commit and begin a family. My instincts had gotten me into trouble in the past, so I accepted that it was time to grow up and commit. Even as I hesitated, that tough-talking voice continued, "Are you going to spend your life looking for the illusion of the perfect soul mate, or the hope of finding a bigger, better deal?" Man, that voice could be crass. But it got to me. Finally, I concluded I'd be an idiot to pass up what was probably a wonderful opportunity and a wonderful woman.

Clearly I was an idiot already. I was approaching thirty and I thought of all my cousins and friends—everybody was getting hitched and raising kids. I'm certainly not a follower, but I just thought, well, something's got to be wrong with me. Why did I not have the same desires as my close friends and family? I was lucky with girls but was I unlucky or unrealistic when it came to the long haul? I also had the pressure of people telling me how perfect Ali was for me and how great we were together. But they didn't know how she and I related one-on-one; they hadn't taken the six-year journey I had. They didn't know everything. The most specific advice I was given came from one of my friends who told me to walk away. He said, "Mario, ultimatums are there to test you. Walk away, man, walk away. That's how they get you. Surprisingly, man, girls can sometimes be a lot more conniving than guys, so beware."

Well, that was no help. The pressure from both sides made me distraught. How to properly decipher my feelings? How was I able to clearly express myself to the right friend, someone who could guide me with wisdom?

Fast-forward one more time. Let me fess up now: the lesson to come is that when your instincts start talking you must be brave enough to listen and clearheaded enough to act on what they are telling you. Of course I wasn't ready to commit wholeheartedly. But I didn't want to listen because I wanted the fairy tale to be true and my instincts to be wrong. I overlooked two very important facts: I wasn't in love with her in the way that she deserved a spouse to be, and, obviously, given all my resistance, I was not ready to settle down.

The lesson, in hindsight, was that I would never keep those sorts of feelings to myself ever again. The nervous hesitation in me should have been shared with her. It wasn't fair to Ali for me not to gracefully tell her how I felt because she was understandably ready for a serious commitment and someone who was ready to jump into marriage with both feet. I also didn't realize that no matter how amazing a person is, no matter how wonderful, if you're not ready, trying to prolong the relationship is pointless.

When they say timing is everything, I don't think it applies to anything more than it does to relationships. Well, maybe timing is a bit more important for landing a jet on an aircraft carrier, but after that, in close second place, are relationships. There have been lots of great women in my life, but I just wasn't ready, for whatever reason, for a long-term relationship.

The problem with the passage of time is that people do change. As far as I was concerned, Ali had changed. The reality was that I had fallen out of love and I wasn't ready, and I confused my unpreparedness with feeling that I wasn't being brave and that all my misgivings were nothing more than cold feet. What's a guy to do in this situation? The worst thing possible: I proposed. I bought the ring and made the engagement official and did so like a zombie.

Even in the midst of proposing, I suppressed my apprehensions. Again, just cold feet, right? I had to man up, I told myself. Repeatedly. If this was what Ali wanted, it was my responsibility to commit. Was walking away worth losing her? No. Then . . . I might as well marry her. Bad logic at the time, I know, but that's the illogical logic I used to make my decision to go forward. I know now that the manliest thing I could have done was to confess my misgivings and take the heat for causing a broken heart, but that wasn't the choice I made.

Then I lost my mind and acted the part of a reformed bachelor. Not only did I go down to Louisiana to propose, but I went even further by asking her father for her hand, hoping that with the family's blessing I would live up to my new role as groom. Her family was very traditional, and with all the emotional gymnastics I'd been through, I hoped this would start us off on the right foot. It was the left foot that got me into trouble.

My buddy Joe organized the bachelor party, complete with his private jet and all my cousins, who'd been planning on our doing a marlin-fishing trip in Cabo San Lucas, Mexico. Joe told me, "Hey, screw that trip. I'm taking care of everything. Grab your cousins. We're going on my plane and we're going to hop around to all the hot spots—Cabo, Puerto Vallarta, Acapulco, and Cancún." It was a seriously generous offer and my crew was game for the adventure.

The bachelor party coincided with college spring break, so it was a far cry from a fishing trip. We started with the hottest spots here in the States—MTV was shooting at many of these locations, so you can only imagine the crowds they drew. Then we jetted off in style to all the Mexican beach resorts. Joe was the man, orchestrating the whole fantasy party from start to end. But what about the women in our lives? Would they approve?

My cousins were all married or in committed relationships, so it was natural for them to ask: "Are we going to tell our wives or girlfriends about this trip?"

My response was, "Yeah, let's just be honest and tell 'em. What are they going to get mad at? It's a bachelor party."

But the group consensus was against me. A resounding "No, we can't tell them" echoed among my friends and *primos*. One cousin was adamant, saying, "If we spring this on them, oh my God, mine will freak out. So let's vote on it."

In the end, I was overruled and we all decided to go hush. Now I was left with another dilemma: I couldn't tell Ali. Again, in hindsight, I know this was the wrong thing to do. The beginning stages of a relationship must be built on a foundation of trust. And trust begins with telling the truth even when it's difficult— especially when it's difficult. Men mature more slowly than women and I imagine Ali was looking at our relationship with more matu- rity than I was at the time. Scratch that. I'm *sure* she was.

That said, I was fine with telling my fiancée of our plans, because it was *my* bachelor party. What did she care where I was going? But I had to keep my mouth shut. We voted not to say anything to anyone and all committed to the white lie that we would be going on a bach- elor party fishing trip. It wasn't as if we'd planned on being bad, but the gang unanimously agreed that their girlfriends and wives would be unnecessarily stressed if they knew where we were headed.

It was a five-day nonstop party. Suffice it to say, my good time was a little too good, because I got inebriated and a little too friendly with a young lady on spring break at one of the stops in some university party town. What was I thinking? At the time, as little as possible! Maybe I'd rationalized it to the point of thinking that the whole Bachelors Gone Wild scene was a rite of passage I was supposed to experience. You know, when in Rome . . . ? The truth is, during those five days, I remember having only vague tinges of guilt. Reality began to settle in, however, when it was time to return home. As time went on, I'd see that the excuse of a bachelor party frenzy wasn't right. The blame, obviously, was my immaturity and inability to keep my priorities in perspective.

Once I took responsibility for my feelings, acknowledging how I had so mishandled my decisions, lightning hit me with truth: I wasn't in love. The thoughts came streaming in, but it was too late. My misgivings reared their ugly heads and I knew I should have broken things off with her before I strayed.

Everything was suddenly crystal clear. But like an idiot I did what you do when you find out you've dug a hole for yourself: I kept digging. I'd tell myself, Oh, whatever, this is my last hurrah, and I'm not married yet so it doesn't count, just one last youthful indiscretion before I step up and become a married man. With that kind of guilty self-defense, I came back and all seemed normal at first. Twitter and other social media were not all the rage, luckily, so what happened wherever it happened stayed there—or so I thought—and I went through the proceedings and got married as planned. I formally walked down the aisle and said, "I do." But in my heart and soul, I was screaming, "I do *not*! I can't! What am I doing?"

When I was at the altar and looked down, I saw my mom and dad with dry eyes. No tears. No emotion. In contrast, four years earlier, when my sister, Marissa, married Kailee Wong—the all-American linebacker from Stanford who began his NFL journey playing for the Minnesota Vikings and then later the Houston Texans—I saw that my parents were visibly moved with tears and expressions of great joy. At my wedding their expressions were blank.

At the reception, Ali and I made the rounds, but you never really talk to anyone at your own wedding. That is, except for the moment when it was time for the traditional dance with my mom. We went out onto the dance floor together and she took both my hands in hers, looked me in the eyes, leaned in so no one could hear, and quietly whispered into my ear, "I hope you know what you're doing, *mijo*. I'm going to pray for you." Mom always knows best and she knew I wasn't ready.

Ali and I didn't get to go on a honeymoon because I was shooting a pilot at the time and I had to do some other work in New York. With that trip behind me, I came back to Los Angeles just in time for the proverbial shit to hit the fan. Ali had found out all about the bachelor party. She brought me into the bedroom and showed me pictures her sister had found. One of our unplanned stops on our bachelor party tour had been at a Louisiana State University spring break party. Ali's sister had a lot of friends at LSU and one of her sister's friends snapped a picture of me in South Padre Island, Texas. I was caught in the white lie. South Padre Island was a far cry from where I'd told her I would be. Not only that, but I was on the stage partying like a rock star with scantily clad girls—certainly not fishing in Cabo. I came clean. No brownie points for me, though. Ali was pissed.

Understandably, she was humiliated—though she sounded more worried about how it would make her look than about our relationship and working things out. She asked me to leave, so I did. At that point, we were not calling it quits so much as putting me in the doghouse and cooling off before figuring out how to make things right. In that short period, she didn't hold back from telling a lot of people what a louse I was. "Louse" may not have been the word. All was starting to become clear. Something was horribly wrong in our relationship and it had to be fixed, immediately.

Then I had an epiphany. I didn't want to save our marriage. The foundation wasn't there. I finally got the balls to say, "I'm sorry. I can't be in this marriage. It's not right for either of us." It was incredibly difficult and heartbreaking for us both. I told her, "I shouldn't have gotten married and I didn't mean to hurt you. I'm sorry." She was hurt and angry, rightfully so. And so two weeks after we said, "I do," we went to the Catholic Church for an annulment.

I take full responsibility for not being mature enough to recognize my own heart in this relationship and for allowing outside pressures to affect my choices. I learned a lot from all of this, which was no solace to Ali or to myself in this mess. I just wasn't ready and my heart wasn't in it. Plain and simple. And I knew that if I ever met someone worth walking down the aisle with, I would make damn sure I jumped in with both feet.

After Ali and I went our separate ways, I regretted most of all that we couldn't find a place of friendship. Almost all of my exes and I became friends after our romantic involvements ended. After all, caring for each other shouldn't stop because you're no longer an item, so why not be friends? Life's too short to bear grudges or carry resentment. That's a lesson that comes with maturity.

The other upshot was reclaiming trust in my own instincts, not only with respect to relationships but also when I next found myself with a new wave of unexpected job opportunities—none of them directly related to hosting.

There are times when you have to be choosy in life and be careful not to overextend yourself. In show business if you do too much, you can also run the risk of becoming overexposed. But when I turned thirty, I resolved to start saying yes to opportunities from all quarters. Saying yes becomes a magnet for more opportunities, as long as you work hard and pace yourself. So the first thing that came along was *The Bold and the Beautiful*.

What did I say? "Yes!"

Doing soap operas is hard. You're given a great deal of dialogue to memorize every day and then entire scenes are shot in one take, maybe two. And it's all happening at a lightning pace. It's like doing theater but with an abnormal amount of dialogue, no rehearsal, and at a really fast tempo. There are some great actors who work in soaps, who hone their craft daily by making all those soapy plotlines feel both real and emotional. Just what the doctor ordered for me at the time. Unfortunately, I had only a one-year deal because they didn't know what to do with my character at the end of my contract, so they just didn't bring him back. He simply disappeared. I was bummed. Fortunately, I'd gotten an opportunity to do another show on the heels of that soap ending: *Nip/Tuck* with Ryan Murphy.

"Yes!" I was stoked. A brilliant writer, director, and producer, Ryan Murphy has done *Glee*, *American Horror Story*, and big feature films like *Eat Pray Love* with Julia Roberts. Shortly after my year on the soap, he offered me a really cool role on *Nip/Tuck* that a lot of people had auditioned for: Dr. Mike Hamoui. My character was supposed to make one of the lead doctors on the show jealous, because the guy I was playing was younger and smarter, not to mention slick, and in better shape. It was the first time I would be naked on film. And in a shower scene with another man in a locker room setting, no less. We were standing there completely naked. Real naked. No loincloth or sock to cover our privates. No banana leaf. Nada.

During production, it wasn't a quick flash of nudity either. We shot for almost eight hours. I was wet for that long too, because we were in the shower. I'm surprised I didn't catch pneumonia.

The other guy was Julian McMahon, and you get to know a guy pretty well when you stand next to him naked for eight hours. We were oblivious to our state of undress after an hour or so. Kind of like in a real locker room. My character turned into a recurring role, through a few seasons, which gave me an opportunity to do some work that was really cool, edgy, and hip—and to be associated with a phenomenal show.

My dating life didn't suffer, but I was trying to say "Yes!" slightly less often to complicated relationships while putting down the pedal on work, my boxing regimen, and the ideas of developing myself as a brand, as Dick Clark had encouraged me to do. If that sounds like I was becoming a monk, I'd better correct the record. It's just that I accepted that there were advantages to being unattached.

During one visit to Las Vegas in these years, when I happened to be in town just blowing off some steam, I unexpectedly crossed paths with a certain mega pop star—who shall remain nameless. The surprise and spontaneity of meeting was strangely not what normally happens in Hollywood. Basically, we had friends in common in Vegas, and I, in party mode, found myself talking to her, enjoying getting to know her as a person. Soon we started with a few drinks, and then, well, both of us being single, there were more drinks, and a lot of laughing and then dancing and more dancing before we threw caution to the wind. As they say, one thing definitely led to another.

That was the night when I was reminded of the advice my cousins used to give about not drinking too much if there was the potential for being amorous on a given night. Unfortunately, I remembered this wisdom too late. And, damn. My cousins were right. From then on I preached the gospel: when out with the ladies, don't drink too much because you never know when you'll be called to duty. Ultimately, in this scenario, I can report that I prevailed, faculties restored—so to speak—even if I wasn't at my best or exactly up to my own standards. But I mean, what are the odds that the one time my cousins' advice turned out to be right happened to be the same night I had my chance with a most desirable pop star? All in all, though, we had a fine time and she was completely awesome. And better yet, she and I retained a friendship that made us both feel good whenever our paths crossed again after that.

What is it about dancing that is so powerful? Well, judging by the next series of unanticipated opportunities, I'd say it's not one thing—it's everything.

In the spirit of saying "Yes!" in 2006—right after I started my four-year run as a recurring guest star on *Nip/Tuck*—I did not say no to the ABC casting folks who had been after me to do *Dancing with the Stars*. This was now the third time that they had approached me. I had always turned them down for a number of reasons. For one, I didn't like the clothes the contestants were wearing—they seemed a little over-the-top and cheesy even. For another, ballroom was not necessarily in my wheelhouse. Sure, I had a little bit of rhythm and had been known to pick up choreography quickly, so I was confident in my skills, but I still wasn't feeling it.

A concern, as I discussed with my agent and manager, was that if I was trying to develop my bona fides as a host, it might blur the lines to be seen as a contestant. That was me trying to think with my brand-conscious hat on.

But when they asked me this third time, my mother, a devoted fan after watching *Dancing* for its first two seasons, decided to play the mom card. She loved the show that much.

"*Mijo*," she said, "listen. They asked you again—please do it. You've got to do it."

Again, my agent and manager were less confident and didn't think it was the right time. But the timing was right in the sense that my other gigs weren't in high gear. And as I thought about it, my instincts kept countering with, "Why not?" Plus, mothers do know best.

On *Dancing*, audiences get to see you as a *person* as well as a TV personality. Instead of working against my brand, I realized that this was a most advantageous platform for letting audiences get to know another side of me—including that competitive former wrestler turned amateur boxer. Could I move? *Sí!* Could I dance? *Sí!* Could I even win? We were about to find out.

Industry hubbub claimed celebs did the show for one of two reasons: to reveal their charisma and distinct personality or to whip out their best dance moves. My feeling is that the first reason is risky. No matter how lovable your personality, if you can't dance, viewers would criticize you anyway. Nor is the contest about athleticism; it's about the dancing—and, of course, being in shape enough to do the moves. So fitness is a plus, but the keys are rhythm, passion, and technique. Certainly, I had the rhythm and passion in my DNA. On technique, I could hope to remember the fundamentals—enough not to embarrass myself.

After much ado, I told my mother that, yes, I was doing the show for her. Once again her positive instincts prevailed, as only the next weeks would reveal.

In the show the celebrity contestants are paired with seasoned ballroom dance professionals. The producers chose to pair me with a charming Russian girl from Ukraine by the name of Karina Smirnoff, like the vodka. This was her first season on the show and, very much like any contestant, she didn't quite know what she was getting into. An incredibly talented dancer, she was new to the pressure of TV, an entirely new animal for her. Karina embraced the philosophy of "Fake it till you make it" and soon thrived on the show, thanks to who she is—smart, worldly, well traveled, and very funny.

We got along right off the bat and we made a great pair, as viewers seemed to agree. When I first met Karina, I was stopped in my tracks by her dark features and exotic beauty. We had instant chemistry when we danced. We learned our routines with ease and came out of the gates killing it. As the judges said on the show, we were one of the strongest dance couples they had seen to date. After our cha-cha, judge Bruno Tonioli said to me, "I've never seen hips move like that. It's like you've got a battery pack in your pants."

Karina and I had the highest scores every single week. All of a sudden, I was deluged with massive public attention like I had never experienced. What? Before long, my face was on the cover of all these magazines and I was making the rounds of the leading talk shows. I couldn't believe how many Americans were fans of the show. It was awesome and sometimes overwhelming.

Truly, though, my run on *Dancing with the Stars* allowed me to bring all sides of myself to the fore, as a performer and as just me. Being myself on camera and showing millions of viewers what I'm about was liberating. Yep, I could now admit, I was a mama's boy, which was why I was doing the show—for my mother and for the family values I cared about. Up until this time, all of that history of being straight outta Chula had been obscured. Now it was part of my public image. Viewers responded with appreciation that I also had nothing but the utmost respect for my partner. I think anytime you have an opportunity to be in front of thirty million people, you're going to make an impression on them. Sometimes it's good, sometimes it's bad, but you can't help but leave a lasting impression if all those people are staring at you week after week. Fortunately, for me, it was a positive imprint.

Karina and I continued to lead in the scoring all the way to the end of the competition. I was working my butt off, training really hard to be the best dancer on that show. The finale came down to two pairs, my team versus Team Emmitt Smith. A football icon, Emmitt Smith was not only the NFL's all-time leading rusher, but he had also played for America's team, the Dallas Cowboys. Emmitt's partner, Cheryl Burke, had started to pull out the stops as we came down to the wire.

This was not a smoker, nothing like getting punched in the face in the ring. It wasn't like boxing at all, nor was it like being out on the one-yard line with Emmitt Smith. If it was like anything, it was akin to having a final audition in front of thirty million viewers and knowing that the winners would be determined by popularity more than any measure of their dancing skills.

Ultimately, the majority of voters gave the win to Emmitt and he was awarded the coveted mirror ball trophy—and more important, the glory. There is no way to sugarcoat the disappointment. A funny thing happens when you go all in, especially with the competitive drive in me and after the intensity of the training and the love we were shown by voters all along. At the same time, coming in second was nothing to apologize for. Regardless, the show completely changed my life from that point on. Later, after the first hundred episodes of *Dancing with the Stars*, the fans and judges voted on who was the top dancer of all time: I got number one!

I would forever be indebted, as if I weren't already, to my mother. If it hadn't been for her, I would never have done the show and none of us could have predicted the ripple effect that it would have on my career. This was a new day and a new dawn in programming after all, and no other platform at the time could have given me a viewership of that scope. The floodgates opened. First there was a savory network development deal, then a movie of the week for ABC Family that became the highest-rated holiday movie ever and still plays every Christmas season, *Holiday in Handcuffs*. I also got a pilot for CBS, which didn't get picked up but was a chance to work with the great Sean Hayes (of *Will & Grace* fame, and so on) and the talented Todd Milliner, writer, producer, and actor. After *Dancing with the Stars*, I also received offers for spokesperson jobs and sponsorships, and continual appearance requests.

Along with a big thank-you to my mother, I also have to really thank my partner, Karina, because she was part of the magic. Oh, and the dance didn't stop after the music ended. Once the show was over, Karina and I dated casually for the better part of two years. We were probably too much alike in some ways—two passionate, artistic types—and that could sometimes make for a volatile relationship. But we also had so much fun together, which was why we were together for so long. Ultimately, we were too combustible together to last and—contrary to rumors flying around toward the end—the truth is we both knew our cha-cha had taken us as far as we were meant to go.

The timing was also such that, at age thirty-five, I was about to receive yet another wild opportunity that came my way straight out of left field.

In early 2008, my manager, Mark Schulman, left me a message to call him back right away. When I did, the connection wasn't great and all I could hear was ". . . Broadway."

Mark Schulman, who bears an eerie resemblance to a cross between a young Billy Crystal and a young Jon Cryer—even though he's convinced that he looks just like Mark Wahlberg—had for the last several years helped to organize my career. Mark usually gives it to me straight, but this time I had to make sure I was hearing him clearly. Had I just heard him say that I was up for a role on Broadway?

Mark paused and then matter-of-factly said, "That's right."

And not just any role—it was the part of Zach, the director, in one of the most iconic musicals in Broadway history: *A Chorus Line.* I was reminded of every dance recital and every school production and live theater piece I'd ever done. Being on Broadway was like that dream you didn't dare acknowledge, because it's like saying, "One day I'm going to climb Mount Everest." "One day I'm going to be on Broadway" was now a dream within my reach.

You know the adage about good news traveling fast? Well, as soon as I accepted the offer to do a six-month run of the show, I was off and running, feeling both excited and nervous, and . . . moving to NYC.

Let's start with the excitement. New York City! If you've got money in your pocket and a decent job, the city is your oyster. And as I was newly single, I was ready for a city that's dating heaven. You can't help meeting new people every day; the streets and restaurants are crowded with people everywhere you go. The city pulses with energy that's like another world compared to my laid-back life back in LA.

I love the lack of artifice in New York. Everybody keeps it real. There are just characters everywhere. Besides their colorful swagger, New Yorkers are also passionate consumers of entertainment and culture. I saw that firsthand when the production put me up in a killer apartment smack in the middle of Times Square. The

Schoenfeld Theatre was on Forty-fifth Street, only a couple of blocks from my condo.

Why was I nervous? Because this was like nothing I'd ever attempted before and everyone in the theater world knew it. The hit revival had been going strong since 2006 and the decision to bring me in to play Zach (as a replacement) was being called a fluke. It turned out that Bob Avian, the show's director, had been talking to my agent about another actor who wasn't available. So my name sort of came up as an offhand possibility. Bob Avian had seen me on *Dancing with the Stars* and followed his gut instinct that, as an actor, I could pull off the intense Zach. From what he had seen, he thought I could hold my own as a dancer and he knew from my earlier career that I had decent singing skills. Avian reported to all the entertainment press that he was so sure I was right for the part, he didn't even audition me. True. But everyone in the Broadway community, supposedly unbeknownst to me, was holding their breath. Was I going to be worth the risk? I had to deliver and I made a promise to myself that I would.

From the minute I arrived at the Schoenfeld and saw all the backstage sights and smelled the accumulated atmosphere of almost a hundred years of theatrical productions, I felt at home. Everyone in the cast was a star. They were incredibly talented; everyone was a triple threat who could sing, dance, and act with a level of skill that was humbling. The same was true of the touring company of the show that was in rehearsal—which allowed me to get up to speed with them before I debuted as Zach. What a privilege and an honor to be among these pros as part of the *Chorus Line* family. They not only helped me raise my game but also validated me as a multifaceted performer, letting me know, "You got this, Mario," and that I was up to par enough to hang with them.

As we readied for the date when I would debut, the cast was supportive and complimentary.

But it was not a walk in the park. Those first few days learning the choreography I had flashbacks to *Kids Incorporated* when the choreographer barked at me for not getting it. However, Bob Avian and the rest of the production team had complete faith in me and never once showed concern, except that only made me more nervous. And that made me work even harder. The show had a grueling schedule. The play itself is intensely physical. You're singing, you're dancing, and you're acting nonstop, and there are no intermissions. On top of all that, *A Chorus Line* ran eight shows a week with only one day dark. This was the big league and the demands definitely kicked my butt.

When the reviews came out after my April 15 Broadway debut, they were almost all raves. Even the snarkier theater reviewers gave me begrudging props, saying besides my performance being quite good that my energy was a welcome addition to the show. Of course there was tremendous excitement from everyone who had banked on me pulling this off. There were so many highs to come from this experience, but I have to say that when some of the cast and I went for drinks at Joe Allen's to wrap up my first week with the show, I felt that I'd made the rite of passage—I belonged.

As you probably know about me and how I was raised, I would never shirk from hard work or from the reality that one should always strike while the iron is hot. So whenever hosting opportunities came up that I could do while I was in New York, I would make the time, no questions asked. Besides, most of the media centers were within walking distance of the Theater District. And then, to complicate my life further, about halfway through my run on Broadway, I landed a great hosting gig on the new MTV show *America's Best Dance Crew*, which the fans called *ABDC*. It was a hot show, very popular on MTV, and a great opportunity to keep my hosting career pumping. To make it all happen, I had to take a red-eye once a week back to LA. I would land in LA, do the show, and turn around and come back to New York on another red-eye. The timing was orchestrated so that I would land and head right into my first show—we had two shows on that day of the week, as it happened. So I was living on virtually no sleep. Whoever knew whomever at the production levels, they managed to arrange a police escort to get me to the condo or the airport because time was so tight. I don't know how they worked out the presidential treatment, but without it I wouldn't have been able to juggle it all. Back at my condo, I would lie down for an hour, get up, do a matinee, go back to my place, try to take another little nap, and have to perform the show again that night. Just as I was catching my breath, the week would fly by and I'd do it all over again. This went on for weeks.

Finally I had some letup when I was just going to be in New York for a while and I was all gung ho, planning for a visit from three of my cousins and a couple of their significant others. Most of all, I was excited to see my cousin Chico, who also happened to be my godson. To him I was Nino—short for *padrino*, or godfather— and in addition to his getting to see the show, I wanted to take him around New York City and be tourists together.

Chico, whose real name was Emilio, had not always had an easy time of it. He was my mom's sister's kid. My aunt was only nineteen years old when she gave birth to him, and she died during childbirth. Everyone was devastated and a dark cloud hung over the family for a long time after that. Doctors said early on that because of all the complications during labor, Chico would most likely be brain-dead or nonfunctional. But he made it; Chico survived. However, he still had some developmental issues—mainly physical, though. For example, he couldn't maintain his balance a lot of the time and would fall often, but he was smart and sharp as a tack.

Chico, five years younger than me, grew up with the knowledge that the reason for his mother's death was that the doctors had given his mom the wrong anesthetic in the delivery room—and so the hospital owed him a large sum of money, payable when he turned eighteen years old. He always saw that money as a beacon of hope that would solve many of his problems. When he finally got his settlement, he was deflated. He had been thinking about it and expecting it for so long, and he thought he'd never have to worry about money again. But it wasn't enough to do that. It was not the cure-all to heal deeper wounds or make up for losses that money can't address.

During the time I'd been away and so busy, I had been concerned about him, to be honest, and wanted to check in with him to make sure he was all set to come visit. We had talked earlier on about him coming out with my cousins Alex and Chica and their respective spouses, and then all of them would stay with me. The rest of the planning was up to me.

A few days before they were supposed to arrive, I called Chico to firm up the details. "You coming, man? You excited? Did you get your plane ticket?"

"Yeah, yeah. I'll be there, Nino. I look forward to seeing you."

Instead of giving him our itinerary, I decided to surprise him and go over it when he arrived.

Cut to: everybody in the group shows up *except* Chico.

What had happened? I looked from cousin to cousin in confusion. "Where's Chico?"

"Dude," Alex explained, "he just flaked out. I don't know. He just didn't come—he didn't call us or anything."

I picked up my cell to call him, but no luck getting ahold of him. I finally asked, "Who was with Chico last?"

Alex apparently had been with him earlier in the week. "Yeah, I took him shopping, for the suit he was going to wear in New York."

The verdict, according to the consensus, was that he'd just decided not to come. But I knew something more serious was up when Alex added, "I'm worried about him. He seems weird lately."

The others went on to explain that Chico had been drinking a lot and he'd gotten a couple of DUIs. Whatever was going on, I assumed part of it was him being immature. I would have never guessed his reckless behavior was a serious cry for help.

A couple of weeks later, I was given the news that Chico had killed himself. He had bought a gun and shot himself in the head. No explanation. No note. Nothing made any sense. He had been fine on the phone with me a few weeks before. He was supposed to come see me in New York. And then, just like that, he decides no. His life is over.

When someone is that broken that they can't see the light, you always question yourself and try to think of anything you could have done. All I kept wondering was, what if he'd come to see me in New York? What if he'd seen that there was life outside of Chula Vista? That the world wasn't so small, and that he wasn't alone? He would have been there in Times Square. We could have gone to Central Park and all the museums. *What if . . .* If he could have come to New York, he would have seen the big buildings, felt the energy, and maybe he would have realized there was something else. If he had been in the city where everyone is a little lonely but everyone is just in this life together, maybe it would have made a difference. I'll never know.

His death made me cry off and on for several days. It's still hard for me to come to peace with it, because it was just so senseless. Six years later, I still haven't erased his number from my cell phone. I can't bring myself to do it.

Something about Chico leaving this world made me want to live in it more fully and more consciously. Another big turning point in my life and a time to reinforce a lasting lesson: Live now for everything you're worth because your life is worth everything.

Toward the end of my run on Broadway, I started to feel a sense of loneliness that had nothing to do with being alone or not. The thing is, I had great East Coast friends who were around and who kept me busy—like Noah Tepperberg, who ran the hottest clubs in the city and was connected to the best restaurants too. With a bevy of models and beautiful people always around him, Noah included me in all kinds of fun scenes and cool parties. But I knew that I was pushing my own limits, burning both ends of the candle. The irony in avoiding being alone was that I ended up going out more, which only had the effect of making me feel lost in the crowd rather than less lonely. Maybe I was homesick for the slower jam of LA or for the family time I loved back in Chula.

Don't get me wrong—I loved being onstage and being part of my *Chorus Line* family. But after curtain call, I'd go back to my dressing room to take off the makeup and realize that I didn't want to go out drinking in the Theater District or cruise the clubs uptown or downtown. Inside I felt strangely hollow. I just didn't have the same desire for the nightlife that I did when I was younger. What was wrong with me? Was I getting old? I didn't necessarily want to settle down and buy a lawn mower and a set of golf clubs, but slowing down a bit was not a bad option for me. Maybe "slowing down" wasn't the goal. Maybe what I wanted was to accept maturity and try a new angle.

Though I couldn't name that tune just yet, I had this new yearning for stability that for someone almost thirty-five years old would not be unusual. The idea of settling down—only just a little—was kind of appealing. I didn't necessarily want to jump into a heavy-duty relationship, but maybe I was ready for a real companion. Nothing in me was thinking about marriage again. I had been down that road once before, and it didn't end well.

If I could hope to have learned from past mistakes, I suppose that my longing for something more—something with substance— was a good sign of maturity. The other sign of growth, I'm happy to report, was that I began to think about what I had to offer in terms of companionship. Financial security was one thing, but as far as stability, who knew where I was going to be from one gig to the next? And commitment? That's not even an easy word for me to type!

That was when—not long before I wrapped *A Chorus Line* for good—I made the decision, once and for all, to commit to what it was that I wanted to do when I grew up. In other words, I was going to commit to hosting all the way. You can't do everything all the time and do everything really well. Of course, I would continue to say "Yes!" to opportunities that helped challenge me in new areas, but the time had come to lay it all on the line and seize the moment to make a name for myself as a host.

Once I had that nailed down, then I could try to solve the Rubik's Cube of long-term relationships. It wasn't that I'd given up on the idea that one day I'd be ready for that kind of commitment. But for the time being that wasn't my priority.

Don't they say that you always find what you need the most just when you stop looking for it? Well, after a few more turning points to come, I was going to find out just how true that is.

CHAPTER 7

# SO YOU THINK
# YOU CAN HOST?

There must be some scholarly research under way at one of our finer educational institutions in this country about whether TV hosts are born or bred. I would not know the answer. Well, I do know that some hosts really and truly seem to be born for the job whereas others attain their hosting skills in other arenas before picking up the mic. And there are others who sort of fall into both categories, which is where I think I fit in. For me, aspects of hosting came naturally, as I found at age eighteen after my very first gig as a host of *Name Your Adventure*. But then, over the years with all kinds of hosting stints, I have continually had to learn new and important skills and tricks of the trade. Contrary to popular opinion about what constitutes a great host, it's not enough to simply enjoy the spotlight and have a gift of gab.

For that reason, actors don't always make the best hosts. On the list of things I had to learn the hard way when starting out as a host was that it's vitally important to take an interest in other people and not to make the conversation all about you. When *you're* the product you've been selling for your entire life, you tend to become extremely self-centered. I call it an occupational hazard because the truth is, when you're in showbiz, you have to be on constant alert as to how you look, sound, and appear to others. At the same time, as a host you still need to bring yourself into the mix in interesting and entertaining ways—because you may sometimes be called on to deliver sound bites to fill the air, so you do need to have some original material.

What I found that helped me on those earlier gigs, like covering sports or hosting beauty pageants and so on, and then being a cohost of a talk show with Dick Clark in my late twenties, is that I love having a platform just to be myself. How cool that there was a job that paid you to be yourself too. Luckily, I've been myself my whole life and am happy with who I am. So hosting just came naturally, whether it was house parties and game nights or, as I later learned, national TV and syndicated radio shows. Another plus for me is that I'm a genuinely inquisitive person, which is a quality that lends itself to interviewing people and carrying a show. Because of that curiosity and wanting to learn and get to know others, I have become a better listener than I might have been at first. And maybe because of the family gatherings at my parents' house when I was growing up, I think like a host most of the time—just wanting to make sure everybody's having a good time. *Mi casa es su casa* would continue to serve me well over time.

Much to my surprise, I've seen hosts on TV who don't pay attention to making guests comfortable and some who don't even listen to the answer from the interviewee before moving on to their next question, or hosts who have no follow-up questions prepared because they haven't been listening. I learned from watching those kinds of examples what *not* to do and I vowed never to be like that. My attitude when I'm interviewing someone is that it's not about me; it's about them. If there is one trait that I've learned really matters, it's that being humble is what makes a host great. For us former child actors who grew up having all that attention, being humble doesn't necessarily come easy. That's why, in hindsight, I value all the jobs that I didn't get for teaching me to be humble—or at least grounded and hopefully real.

*Dancing with the Stars* proved to be an intensive primer for staying humble. And, again, it put me on the radar for a lot of producers looking for hosts who would attract a large viewership—just as it unexpectedly helped land me a top spot in a Broadway musical.

Actually, a year or two before I was cast as Zach in *A Chorus Line*, I had already set my sights on finding the right hosting job that I could make my own. The reality, as I surveyed the landscape, was that there were not many daily entertainment newsmagazine shows in which I could see myself potentially hanging my hosting hat for a while and where the content would fit well with my skill set. Though I'm a news junkie and could have pursued an anchor job, my background was entertainment and that was where my heart was leading me. But when my talent reps reached out to see whether any of the top entertainment news shows were hiring, only one of them—*Extra*—responded that it might have a possibility for its weekend edition.

As my luck would have it, *Extra* was my number one choice. I liked the format, how the show was put together, and how they kept special segments fresh and a little different from the competition. Obviously, I had a good amount of hosting experience by this point, but I knew that I would have much to learn about how they ran the weekend entertainment show. They called me in to test, and fortunately they loved me—and I loved them.

The great news when I took *A Chorus Line* was that I was able to continue my fledgling relationship with *Extra* in New York City as a correspondent doing interviews for the weekend show. The studio was on Forty-fourth Street, a hop, skip, and jump from my condo and the theater. Crazy and sleep deprived as those months were—what with being in a Broadway show, flying back and forth to LA to host MTV's *America's Best Dance Crew*, and my New York *Extra* work—I loved the opportunity to prove myself. Eventually, after paying my dues as a correspondent, I segued officially into being cohost of *Weekend Extra*.

Much of the time, I simply stood there and read a teleprompter. The challenge was to make it sound conversational and lively. Sometimes there were glitches and I would have to ad-lib, which made me feel like Will Ferrell as Ron Burgundy—making it up on the spot. But it wasn't as if they would really need me to think on my feet or provide long, run-on banter with my cohost—the very sweet, cool, and spunky Tanika Ray. We got along great, had fun, and simply had to report the news of the weekend from the entertainment world.

Unlike with other hosting gigs I had undertaken in the past, the *Extra* host wasn't there to offer clever opinions or filler in these small blocked-out moments. This wasn't because the executive producers were against us showing personality but more because many viewers nowadays have short attention spans—and so many options calling out for their eyeballs—that if we didn't keep up the frenetic pace, people might change the channel. That was a whole new aspect to the learning curve that I hadn't fully grasped earlier.

When *Extra*'s senior executive producer Lisa Gregorisch-Dempsey had first called me in to meet with her about the potential for a full-time hosting job, I was well aware that she held the reins of power and that whatever she decided would be pivotal to my career. Before I'd gotten there, Mark McGrath, former singer of the band Sugar Ray, had become the host of the daily weekday show. My understanding was that he was thinking about going back to music and might be giving up the big chair he'd been holding down. So I wanted a shot. When I met with Lisa, I made that clear, but she wasn't convinced. She's incredibly tough and smart, and doesn't pull any punches. Let's put it this way: I would later give Lisa Gregorisch-Dempsey the affectionate nickname "Carmela"—in homage to Edie Falco's character on *The Sopranos*. At that point in our discussions, Lisa wanted to keep me as host of the weekend show—perhaps because she didn't think I was ready for the daily or maybe she thought my vibe was too young. But very quickly, perhaps as the worker bee in me tried to go above and beyond in my weekend hosting duties, I must have proven that I could perform well in the big leagues. Finally, shortly after I left New York and returned to Los Angeles, I was asked to be the sole host for daily *Extra*. Full-time!

As fast as it happened, the journey to find my hosting home had really begun almost eight years earlier when Dick Clark challenged me to set my sights on this kind of opportunity. Not only did I find that home, I knew right away that it was where I belonged. There was an immediate family atmosphere on *Extra* and it reflected the professionalism of everyone who was part of the team—we all felt the drive to go beyond the call of duty and to make each other look good, and to grow together as a show. Not long after I came in as host in 2008, we outgrew the Victory Studios, where our offices would remain while we relocated our studio and filming location to the fabulous Grove, an outdoor mall with shopping, dining, and entertainment, plunked down in the heart of Hollywood, where the world famous Farmers Market still exists. As one of the two shows produced by Warner Bros. and leased to NBC Universal Television—along with the talk show *Ellen* with my girl, the sensational one and only Ellen DeGeneres—*Extra* embarked on such a period of growth that we would move yet again.

And that's how we arrived at our current shooting location at Universal Studios Hollywood. Imagine going to work every day at a legendary film studio that's also a theme park with rides and entertainment and, oh, that is also the home of Universal CityWalk—some of the best stores, movie theaters, and restaurants on the planet.

Hosting *Extra* absolutely turned out to be the dream gig that I'd been looking for—a spot in the crow's nest that would let me stay at the forefront of entertainment news on the best show in the business. We recently celebrated our twentieth year on air, five of which (soon to be six) I was on board. Every day is my own *Name Your Adventure*!

In fact, one of the big aha moments that I had in the early days of hosting *Extra* was that it's great to be a fan, to get excited the way kids allow themselves to do—whether it's behind the mic on the red carpet for the best awards shows like the Oscars and the Grammys or at a movie premiere or at a charity gala. Why hide the excitement? That doesn't mean being one of those fawning fans. Rather, it's showing some love that you naturally would when getting to meet many of the coolest people in the world.

Are there ever times when I am such a fan that I've gotten nervous interviewing stars? The answer is no, not in recent years. The only time I ever got really nervous to meet any celebrity was long before I was a host, when I was a kid, and I met Hulk Hogan for the first time. Hulk Hogan was an inspiration, a figure I loved and wanted to emulate all those years, so even as an adult I get a retrospective tingle when I see him. "There's the Hulkster!" I was a Hulk-o-maniac!

I learned that what helps take away the nerves is that a host has to be a kind of expert in following the television, film, and music worlds closely. So when I'd meet all these talented individuals very much at the top of their game, I'd be prepared to be on top of mine. Some of that came naturally, but I had to master the prep work of knowing in advance what to ask, whether my questions related to biographical details or events tied to the past or to current projects.

For example, if you had the chance, what would you ask your favorite actor, rock star, or reality celebrity? In honing my approach over the years, I've had the thrill of getting to do that every day and have had fascinating conversations in the process. Another personal preference I've discovered is to try not to have interviews per se, but to have genuine conversations. So that's where being a fan— yet also being a peer—can help. Maybe because I've been in front of the camera for so many years, and famous people I interview know that I grew up in the business, they treat me like one of their own. Whatever the case may be, they feel comfortable with me and, just between us, they end up divulging a lot more than they probably want to in our interviews.

For viewers, this is big value added, because that kind of approach lets the audience in on details and emotion they wouldn't get in other interviews—unless, of course, they are being interviewed by the likes of Matt Lauer or the great Barbara Walters, who is one of the very best at encouraging celebrities to open up and be themselves.

The other hosting trait that's a learned skill is an understanding of the clock. A celebrity, whether in the midst of promoting a movie, record, or book, has only so much time and can't talk to everyone. Besides, nobody in entertainment has time for just shooting the breeze forever, so the job of the host is to move the conversation along in a fast, celeb-friendly, but meaningful way. Everyone appreciates the effort and it's no accident that stars love *Extra* for that—which, of course, makes it that much easier when we see them at press junkets for movies, on the red carpet, or in the studio where we shoot the show daily. There are a few major entertainment shows that monopolize the airwaves, but because of the Internet and a million cable channels, there has been an onslaught of people waving around microphones, recording devices, and still photo cameras claiming they need sound bites to promote a project. Publicists for celebrities, therefore, very carefully pick and choose which host and what outlet will have the most promotional value. There are so many domestic outlets for entertainment that it can make people crazy. Not to mention all the international press they already have to do. My point is that publicists and celebrities alike love *Extra*—and that makes my job easy. Or shall I say, *easier?*


One of the frequently heard truisms in Hollywood is that the biggest stars are usually the nicest and the most gracious toward entertainment media. I'd heard that in my early part-time hosting flings but hadn't confirmed it until I started hosting full-time. Sure enough, the A-list stars—whether I've met them at events or been able to interview them for *Extra*—are not just cool and often down-to-earth but tend to be generous with their time. Then again, they are actors, so maybe they're acting nice. It doesn't matter either way, does it? If they're smart enough to fake being nice, then they deserve the good reputation. The challenge for the interviewer with the bigger stars is to learn how to be something of a psychologist and know what you have to offer them in return for their willingness to talk to you and your mic. If I can ask a question that leads a celebrity to an answer he or she has never thought about, or to tell a story that he or she loves to tell, that's a win-win.

Earlier, in learning the hosting ropes, I was sometimes reluctant to meet the superstars I most admired for fear that they might turn out to be a jerk—and that would just crush me. How could I do my job in bringing out their best if they had just shattered the image that I'd loved about them? It did happen on a few rare occasions and I couldn't go back to the movie or the song that I used to love. Fortunately, most of the people that I had always wanted to meet turned out to be even cooler than I'd imagined. It made me even a bigger fan when that happened.

Tom Cruise, Will Smith, Denzel Washington, Hugh Jackman, and Sandra Bullock are the epitome of genuine people who I know to be really nice too and gracious with their time. There's a secret that I figured out after a while about how the top stars walk that fine line between holding on to their privacy yet being available for interview. How? In the most honest and masterful way they can, they will take charge of the interview. They will make you as a host/interviewer feel as special as you want to make them feel.

For example, Al Pacino. His iconic roles as Michael Corleone in *The Godfather* or Tony Montana in *Scarface* are enough to make anyone a fan, and those are only two of the films from a long list of hits throughout his career. He is more than a star and an icon in my book. Not only did he live up to my expectations, but he was the first to approach me on the red carpet.

"Hey, Mario," he said, in his New York Italian voice as he came over to me. "How you doing?"

"Whoa," I responded. "You know who I am?"

"Are you kidding? I loved the show you did with Dick Clark," Al said. *"The Other Half."*

"Really?" I replied. "That was years ago."

We both laughed and I couldn't believe it. That was a great moment in my television hosting life, that's for sure. But as the conversation turned to him, we were conversing like old friends. An extremely warm person, he clearly didn't carry a lot of pretense about him. Yet he made an even bigger fan out of me that day and gave me a great interview.

Another example: Cher. Let me count the ways. Cher, also an icon, is one of the most multidimensional stars to light up the world of entertainment. I admire her as an artist because she has never limited herself to only one arena. She says "Yes!" to work: from her music/variety TV show to everything she's done as a recording artist and concert performer who is still going strong, to all of her unforgettable film roles. Like Pacino, she too came up to me at a recent event before I was set up to talk to her. In that distinct Cher voice, she casually asked, "Mario, hey, what's up? I just saw you on HGTV. You remade your garage."

That was hilarious. Of all the things she could have seen me on . . . HGTV turning my garage into a gym! How random. After that, Cher and I could talk about anything and everything. But that's what the top stars do—they do their homework as well.

Then again, we all have bad days and even the most successful celebs do too. And some of the A-listers can just be jerks, although I've never been able to figure out why. They have so much that other people don't have, so you'd think they should be appreciative and gracious. It's not so much that they are rude; it's just that if you veer ever so slightly away from their prepared talking point, they act as if you've violated their privacy.

Not long ago, I was interviewing a celebrity who is close with Mila Kunis and I asked something benign about whether she was happy to hear that Mila and Ashton Kutcher were having a baby. She preferred not to comment, she said sternly, responding in a way that made it seem as if I had some nerve to ask about her happiness for other celebrities. To be honest, I've gotten weird looks from some stars when I've asked questions as basic as "How're you doing?"

Part of the problem is the time we're living in, when every lit-tle comment can become magnified a million times over on social media. Still, a reaction of "What do you mean, how am I doing?" or "Happy? You want to know if I'm *happy*?"—in not so many words—can be discouraging to an entertainment host.

Of course, from what I know of human nature, not all actors are outgoing and comfortable out of character. Many are shy or have real insecurities that give them the inner life from which to draw on in emotional performances. Some use their aloof intensity in building their brands. I remember thinking that about Ray Li-otta when I met him at a boxing championship fight—Sergio Mora versus Peter Manfredo. I'd been sent by NBC to cover celebrities and VIPs who were there as fans of boxing. As Ray was sitting in a prime spot—next to the aisle at a corner of the ring—I asked him for a comment or two on the fight.

I'd been a huge fan of Ray Liotta from the time I was a kid and watched him in his breakout role in Martin Scorsese's *Goodfellas.* So, naturally, I was excited to tell him that, as well as talk boxing. Ray looked at me with those intense blue eyes for less than a second and then declined, saying, "I don't really do that kind of thing, sorry." Sure, I understood, but it was really a simple request in a loose environment that would have endeared him not only to me and the NBC folks but to all the fight fans watching.

Let down, I felt like an autograph seeker who gets a no from a celebrity. While I know that stars, like all of us, can have bad days, Ray was, after all, having a drink and getting ready to watch an exciting fight. How bad could that be?

Along those lines, I had an eye-opening experience while at-tending a VIP reception that included Tiger Woods. Part of the small group in the room included Darius Rucker, the lead singer of Hootie and the Blowfish, and he and I talked for a while. There were very few people in the room—not many more than fifteen—so Tiger was not inundated with fans. Because of that, one of my buddies who was there with me thought it would be easy for me to ask Tiger to let him take a picture.

I first said, "Nah, I don't want to ask for a picture. We're cool right here."

But my buddy kept pushing it. He reminded me that Tiger had seen me hanging with Darius, so I could ask and not come off as a pushy fan type. Without making it a big deal, I could ask for a shot of the three of us—as would be expected in a reception like that.

Why not? I agreed and diplomatically went over to Tiger and told him how much it would mean to my friend if we took a quick picture together. I had the camera out, ready to go, with my pal standing by too. It would have taken two seconds.

Tiger thought about it and then said, "Um, you know, I really don't feel like taking pictures right now. But tell you what—how about a handshake instead?" Really? He took longer to answer than it would have taken to just say, "Sure, take a picture, and thank you."

For a beat, I looked back at him with confusion draped across my face. Then I just laughed and said, "Ha ha. Don't worry about it, man. All good."

Inside, however, I was steamed. Why was a handshake preferable to a photo? Did he think we were going to make copies and use his likeness for profit? Did he not want us to have a keepsake that would mean something? Who knows? I do know that when I turned around to walk away, I couldn't help mumbling something aloud about what a jerk he was. Or words to that effect. No skin off my back, but that was sort of a textbook "How not to be gracious" moment. I must have told this story two hundred times.

When a short time later he was the brunt of *Saturday Night Live* skits and late-night TV jokes over the breakup of his marriage, I didn't feel sorry for him, because payback's a bitch. He lost two fans from the incident—not that he's losing sleep over that. Still, it's not hard for a star to fall from grace, for an abundance of reasons. There is no payoff for not being nice, bad days and needs for privacy notwithstanding.

That said, I am not paid by *Extra* to rate stars on their niceness or lack thereof, so as a host I have learned to roll with whatever the celebrity needs or wants. And if that star isn't offering a friendly "Hey, Mario, I saw you hosting *X Factor* last night," well, no biggie. Thick skin turns out to be very useful to a host. At press junkets I have found this to be particularly true. There is one music star, to remain nameless, who made it clear he did not want to talk to me directly—as explained to the publicist, even when I was sitting only two feet away. The nameless music star actually said, "Will you tell Mario that I want to talk about my new album?" Then the publicist would say, "Mario, he wants to talk about his new album." Two feet away, I replied, as if I couldn't hear him, "You got it!"

For most hosts, I've found, the more difficult celebs are usually in the much larger pool of those who are stuck on the middle rung of celebrity—what the industry calls the B-listers. It's not that they're downright rude (though they sometimes can be), but basically they treat you, the host, in a dismissive "What's your name again?" way. The B-listers can be tough, as can the C-listers, the kind who complain at awards shows how they didn't get their gift bag—the one that's full of fun free swag—and then they end up leaving with three swag bags. There is also another group that has a bad rep among hosts: reality stars. Some of these newly anointed celebs have bad attitudes. You can sense their "Do you know who

I am?" mentality the second they walk into the room with their unearned sense of entitlement that is often palpable. Occasionally, I have found myself thinking, Buddy, if I'm talking to you next year, man, am I going to be surprised!

The awareness that has helped put all this in perspective is that as a host, most days I can't and don't think of myself as a celebrity—that's part of staying humble and grounded. There are no delusions of grandeur when the celebrities I interview are much more famous than I am. That comes from interviewing some of the biggest and most influential figures in Hollywood day in and day out. Some of the people I interview are so famous they can't leave their homes without being hounded by fans or paparazzi. When they show up to be interviewed on *Extra*, they arrive laden with security and surrounded by an entourage. I have some of that, to be sure, Chula Vista–style. But in comparison, the paparazzi rarely harass me and my days are not filled with scouting safe places to go have quiet dinners. And I'm more than thankful for that.

"So you've got a beef with Russell Crowe?" I began, warming up for an interview with George Clooney during an awards season press junket.

Always super cool and gracious with me, Clooney is a total throwback type, a modern-day Clark Gable. I admire the fact that he's not only a former TV actor, but he also paid his dues and didn't really gain fame until his midthirties.

"Me? No, he's the one with the beef," George replied with a laugh, reminding me that Russell Crowe had called him out for being a "Frank Sinatra wannabe."

This was one of those countless instances where research can make or break an interview. For me, research is as important as the wig. I read everything I can about the projects, the producers, directors, writers, actors, and actresses and whatever else I can find to be ready for an off-topic question during scheduled and unscheduled interviews. I research celebrities' dating histories, their current relationship status, whether they're single, married, just broke up, just had a baby, or "it's complicated." From Wikipedia to *Entertainment Weekly* to sports and music magazines and more serious journalistic pieces, I try to scour the Web and the newsstand to read everything I can, soak up as much information of interest as possible, put it all away, and then just have a conversation. These are usually stories already covered in the press, so if I bring them up, it's not as if I'm gossiping. In fact, celebrities have talked to the press already and are mostly happy to give comments that maybe haven't been reported before. If I've done my homework and read the information, I'll retain it—like the story about the beef Russell Crowe had with Clooney.

"Well, what about you and Leonardo DiCaprio in Mexico?" The story I'd read had alleged that while in Mexico there was a pretty intense basketball game that Clooney and his older group of friends had against DiCaprio and his younger crew. Apparently the young guns were talking trash and being a bunch of punks, so Clooney and his guys stepped it up and schooled them. "So, George, what's the real story?"

George said, "Yeah, Leo's buddies were being a little mouthy and show-offy." He added that it was a lot of fun beating team Di-Caprio. Clooney and the older dudes won in three games, and in one game skunked 'em eleven to zero.

Yep, research is golden—that I have learned. Without preparation, you are asking for embarrassment. As a case in point, I once went to do a one-on-one interview with Ben Affleck after missing the screening of the film he starred in. My excuse was that I'd been stuck in traffic that night because of a bad accident, so I never saw the movie. But the studio sends out screeners and I could have made the effort to watch the film, except that another series of unfortunate conflicts came up that night. Instead of being honest, I chose to wing it—read that as "fake it."

Here is a hint about how it went: Ben Affleck is a poker player—an avid poker player—and my guess was that he would probably see right through me.

We started talking about poker, ironically. That went well, or so I told myself as I tried to play it cool, still nervous and embarrassed. With a surge of confidence, I kicked off the point of the interview by sitting down in front of him and saying, "Great job on the film!"

Ben nodded and waited for me to say what specifically I liked and then I knew he was too good a poker player to fall for that. My inner monologue could have been up in print with a thought bubble that said, "He's reading me. He's reading me. He can see that I'm lying!" Of course, he did a great job, but I didn't know that because I hadn't seen the movie. Though I forged on, asking general enough questions and hoping he might not pick up on the ruse, I wasn't sure I pulled it off.

Not a disaster, but it was just awkward and uncomfortable. Bottom line: I didn't do my job well and the interview wasn't great. From then on, I made it a policy not to do the interview if I haven't seen the project.

I should note that a requisite skill for hosts is to learn to ask questions that are more than just softballs. It is, after all, entertainment news and the ability to touch on controversy can lead to lots of attention on social media and increased viewership. That means part of my homework is reviewing questions I *must* ask during an interview, usually per the producers.

Even though we try to make it look spontaneous, many of the questions you see reporters asking on TV aren't thought up on the spot; they're well planned, albeit sometimes boring. The producers at *Extra* often craft the questions they want me to get in and then I make them my own. During a recent red-carpet prep, for example, I was asked to bring up a comment having to do with the reality TV show *The Bachelor.* The show and the comment had nothing to do with the awards show, but it was topical. Apparently the winner of *The Bachelor* had asserted that he didn't think a gay version of the series would be a good idea. The media had grabbed hold of that and were having a field day with it. So when I was interviewing the celebrities on the red carpet, I not only had to ask them about the awards show, the movies, and their outfits, but I also had to work in questions about that comment. The producers typically ask me to take advantage of the opportunity because it's not easy to get a microphone under the noses of some of these A-list celebs and that sound bite could be used in another story.

Helping generate the show's provocative content is part of my job description and I don't think that's a bad thing. It's just that some days that's easy and some days it's uncomfortable. My personal preference is to ask questions only about the matter at hand and not stray from that. Yet that's not reality. It can get tricky to ask something out of left field that's obviously intended for controversy. Imagine you're getting your car fixed and the mechanic asks you about your underwear. It's that out of place. So when I have to ask these questions, it puts me in a really weird position. Sometimes the celebrities give you a look like, "Huh? Are you serious?"

Much as I don't like it, I feel the heat from the producers looking for the sound bite. And they want something that is relevant to whatever the big story of the day is. Of course, I do my best to ask in a smooth way to finesse the situation, but some of the inquiries are so out in left field no amount of panache will ease the tension. As an example, at the 2014 Screen Actors Guild Awards preshow, I had to ask an awkward question to every person of color. My producers wanted me to get their reaction to the latest Madonna controversy that was all over the Twitter-sphere and involved her referring to her white son as "my little N-word."

So, I'm standing on the red carpet and here comes Oprah, who's been nominated for a SAG Award for her work in *The Butler*. I hadn't seen her in a while, but I admire her for countless reasons, among them her meteoric rise to the upper stratosphere of hosting. As she approaches me, I catch sight of her big smile and I am painfully aware in the back of my head that my producers want me to ask her, "How do you feel about Madonna's using the N-word in reference to her son? She said she did it in a loving way, but is it ever acceptable?" Talk about an awkward position. Everyone's in a jovial mood and wants to talk about their movie and the awards, but the producers want me to ask that! Sure enough, she steps up to the camera, and as soon as I welcome her, they're bugging me about it. I'm congratulating her on the film, saying happy birthday and talking about some pictures of her hanging out with the First Lady, just trying to make small talk before I drop the bomb.

And then I have to ask the question because my producers are glaring at me. So I hit her with it. And the look of shock on her face is painful. This must be the first time she's heard about it. Her eyes get really big. I am literally breaking the news to Oprah!

And then she processed it. Just as she started to answer me, Oprah said, graciously, "You know what, Mario? Let's move on to the next question. This is a little too touchy. I don't feel it's the right spot for this, and I don't want to go anywhere near it." What else could I say to her but, "Okay, I respect that. I understand. Thank you." And then I went immediately back to her movie.

But talk about uncomfortable, talk about weird. Lee Daniels, the director of the film, was standing right there, and he sort of rolled his eyes and said, "Oh, next! Come on, Mario!" And I felt like screaming, "Hey, I don't want to talk about this stuff! My producers are trying to get some sound bites."

The truth is, all entertainment news shows do it. So do local and national news outlets that cover aspects of entertainment. Everyone in media is on the hunt for newsy moments. But you can imagine how I must feel as I'm asking every gay person their reaction to *The Bachelor* and I'm asking every person of color their reaction to the Madonna thing. Yikes.

No show is perfect; it's TV. So there are always flubs and bloopers from us messing up. I find human error funny whenever we're on the red carpet. All the awards shows are feeding frenzies but the Oscars top them all. That's where the media really doesn't get any space—we're stationed around a prickly hedge, literally squished up next to it, left standing there for four hours straight.

You're also inevitably standing next to somebody from *USA Today*, *The Hollywood Reporter*, or some French magazine—with the red carpet three feet in front of you and you're behind a hedge leaning forward. I was once poked in the crotch of my tuxedo with these branches going through my pants while I was trying to talk to Tom Hanks. Not fun. It's very tight quarters there behind the hedge; they pack us in like sardines. There is often pushing and shoving and tempers flaring. I remember one time our producer Jeremy Spiegel got into it with one of the French magazine people, right in front of Kevin Spacey and Jack Nicholson. Kevin Spacey acted as the referee and was trying to calm things down. He said,

"Hey, hey, you guys, take it easy." The celebrities were calming down the producers and reporters! It felt like I was on a *Jerry Springer* episode.

Then again, any time there's drama on the red carpet it's exciting. I think the tension builds because all the "cool kids" come at the end and there is so little time left to get in your questions. Everyone in the lineup waits for all the big stars: Brad Pitt, Angelina Jolie, Sandra Bullock, Oprah. All those people come at the very end and they all come at the same time. We're left with a conundrum: Sandra Bullock doesn't want to wait for Julia Roberts to finish her interview with you, and Brad Pitt and Angelina will wait for no one. And so you're kind of scrambling. It's a delicate dance. You never want to blow anybody off to talk to a bigger star. I always try to be respectful and mindful of finishing my conversation and I just get to the next person when I get to them. And hopefully they'll still be there. I don't want to blow anyone off; I think it's mean and unnecessary.

All the other awards shows—the SAGs, the Golden Globes, the Grammys—provide a platform for us to stand on, so we have a little bit more space and it's much more civilized. However, the rule of thumb is that all the big names come in during the last few minutes on the red carpet. If it's the Grammys, inevitably Paul McCartney and Jay-Z and Beyoncé will all arrive right at the end. That's why I have to be on my toes and be prepared.

You know how my mom always wanted to keep me busy so I wouldn't have time to get into trouble? Hosting full-time for *Extra*—with Carmela Soprano (aka our executive producer) keeping me in line—is sort of a grown-up version of keeping really, really, really busy and out of trouble.

And in keeping with saying "Yes!" to opportunities, I leapt at the chance to host *The X Factor* with Simon Cowell and crew. Because of my schedule at *Extra*, they knew going in that I wouldn't be able to rehearse the show before taping. But in what turned out to be a trial by fire, they trusted that I was the host who could pull off a great show without a rehearsal. I did literally every episode of *X Factor* completely cold. No rehearsal. And we're talking about a major production show that's shot at CBS TV studios. Talk about a crash course in all manner of hosting challenges, except it all went like clockwork because of the precision of Simon Cowell. Far from the caustic critic he appears to be, Cowell is actually super cool once you get to know him—a real gentleman. He's far and away the best judge—ever—in the history of talent competition shows.

Cowell does run a very tight ship and he has great staff working for him. From the standpoint of an entrepreneur, Simon Cowell is a role model as well. He's polite, savvy, fair, and approachable to employees and fans alike.

We end up talking about music a lot when we're just hanging out. I loved having the chance to ask him, "Who do you think the American version of the Beatles are?" I told him my pick was the Eagles. He agrees with me there and thinks maybe Aerosmith is a strong second. Of course, he thinks all the best acts are from the UK and it's hard to argue with him when you think about such giants as Led Zeppelin, the Rolling Stones, and Black Sabbath. One of the things that surprised me about him is how supportive he is. He would sometimes leave messages on my phone when he thought we had a really good show and thought I did a good job. He's just that kind of guy. For a boss who is infinitely busy to take the time—I love that. While it's true that he has got more money than he knows how to spend nowadays, I don't think money is what motivates him. He loves discovering talent and providing the platform for the world to recognize up-and-coming performers; he loves being a presence that encourages people to believe in themselves and work toward their dreams.

If I ever worry that I've overloaded myself, I have only to look at Cowell. Though I was sorry when *X Factor* was canceled, I have been around long enough to know how these things play out. My fingers are crossed that I have a role to play on whatever show Simon Cowell develops next. And I can't wait to interview him about it on *Extra*.

I n the entertainment media world, the most strenuous hosting assignment in my view is working a press junket.

A junket, as it is known in Hollywood, is an event that's designed to bring as much media as possible to one location to cover the release of whatever is being launched or promoted. In moviedom, junkets allow the major studios the opportunity to utilize the star power of the release's most celebrated actors and directors to help promote a film. These are stars who are considered the most bankable because they have the ability to draw the most amount of public interest that will bring in the bank at the box office. They are indispensable once the publicity gears have been set into motion.

A junket lasts only a day and is usually held in a five-star hotel in a major city or cities. It is planned with militaristic precision once a movie is complete and ready to be shipped out to a "theater near you." So the junkets are strategically staged to gather the media in major cities around the world, with reporters flocking in from all over to fawn over the film's stars and ask redundant questions in a sit-down interview.

For films like *Transformers* and animated movies like *Ice Age*, the studios might spend over a million dollars on a couple of days of press junket events. Imagine that! Not to mention the same amount they spend in other cities and in foreign countries if they think the location will add to the promotional value. I saw a junket for *Fast Five* in Brazil, and Tom Cruise did his *Mission: Impossible—Ghost Protocol* junket in Dubai. Studios will even sometimes pick up the tab to fly in media when they really want to capture the attention of the moment. The more they expect the film to make, the more they will spend on promoting it. Why? Because fanning the flames of excitement through media is going to create the buzz and excitement that will allow the movie—or the album that's dropping or the book that's launching—to "open." A failure to do well in the opening week can kill a great project in its tracks. It's high-stakes gambling time and a successful junket is hugely important.

In the luxury hotels where the junkets are typically held, entire floors are sequestered off from the rest of the public. *Extra* will usually set up in its own room in the hotel and we use our personal camera crew; other times the movie has its own camera crews set up for each of the participating stars. For example, let's take the amazing film *12 Years a Slave*. At that junket, I walked down the hallway in the hotel and would see the names Chiwetel Ejiofor, Brad Pitt, Michael Fassbender, Paul Dano, Lupita Nyong'o, and Steve McQueen written on pieces of paper taped to the various doors. The interviews with the stars or the director take place inside those rooms, while outside those doors are three or four chairs where reporters wait in line to have their four minutes with the star. The junket's organizational team literally uses a stopwatch, and when your time is up they kick you out of the room and it's on to the next reporter.

Compared with other folks waiting in line, I imagine my junket experience is a bit different because I've met many of the stars prior to this incredibly abbreviated sit-down interview. When I walk in and see the star sitting waiting to be interviewed, several things go through my head: I wonder how tired they are; I hope I don't forget my questions; I hope I have enough time to ask all the questions on my list; and, most important, I genuinely hope we can have a laugh and make the process painless and fun for us both.

There's a camera crew there, two chairs, and the big players. On the same day that I interviewed George Clooney on a junket for the film *The Monuments Men* (and worked in those questions about his basketball game with DiCaprio), I went on to do interviews with Matt Damon and Cate Blanchett, obviously great actors, and both passionate about work they do outside of their comfort zones. That was the same junket when I met and interviewed Bill Murray for the first time. He is as cool and funny in person as he is embodying all those characters he does. Bill Murray, by the way, is a lot taller than you would think—he's about six-four. He came in to our interview wearing pink pants, a pink shirt, and half a beard. After chatting a bit about his role in the movie, he volunteered that he was staying at George Clooney's house for the junket.

"George is a great guy," I said, nodding.

Bill Murray shrugged and said, with a twinkle in his eyes, "Except that he's a compulsive cheater in basketball."

Hmm. Note to self: remember to requestion Clooney about the DiCaprio story.

"Really?" I asked Murray.

According to Bill Murray, George Clooney is not good at basketball. They were apparently playing one-on-one and Murray could have easily killed Clooney, but "I decided to let him win because I was his houseguest and wanted to be polite."

You can just picture his deadpan delivery as he's saying this. I have to give it up to Bill Murray—he's a guy who plays by his own rules in Hollywood, including the fact that he doesn't have an agent or a manager. If you want Bill Murray, you have to call an 800 number. That goes for everyone. Apparently, you leave your address where the script can be picked up. And if he reads it and likes it, you get a call back. That's how you get Bill Murray in your movie. Everyone—including Steven Spielberg and Martin Scorsese—has to call in on the same 800 number. No favoritism allowed.

Other junkets that stand out for me include interviews with Jennifer Lawrence, who is one of those wonderful young stars who keep it real. She's such a sweetheart and so down-to-earth. She freaked out when she first met me during a junket for *Winter's Bones* because she was a huge fan of *Saved by the Bell*. She hopped out of her chair and brought her brothers into the room to introduce them to me. I guess her family members were big fans of *Saved by the Bell* too. How do you not love a star who can be a fan too?

That attitude, I have to say, is more widespread than not. Most people in show business who have gained any kind of a foothold work very hard at what they do, so why not find ways to make the work fun? Certainly that's the atmosphere I like to create as a host. Not long ago I hosted a Katy Perry special that came about because of my business relationship with Clear Channel. This project was to be aired on the CW Network. The special included her live concert presented sort of like VH1's *Behind the Music*. Katy and I hung out for two hours, and when she wasn't performing we did interview questions. It didn't feel like work at all. I've had her on *Extra* a bunch of times and also on my radio show—one of my more recent exciting ventures. Katy Perry is one of the biggest pop stars in the world and I can honestly say that she's down-to-earth. She always sticks her fingers in my dimples when we see each other and has told me that her mom and grandmother love me.

Compliments from Jennifer Lawrence and Katy Perry are genuinely flattering. It's also nice to know that we've got a comfortable enough relationship that makes it easy to pick up the conversation the next time an interview opportunity rolls around.

As someone who has climbed the ladder and as an outside observer, I'm fascinated by how celebrity does or doesn't change people as they make their way up the ranks of Hollywood fame. Take Taylor Swift. I can remember seeing her perform at small-town carnivals and then big state fairs. She has managed to remain the nice girl I first met.

Bruno Mars is a phenom who seemingly came up fast from obscurity to superstardom although that is rarely the case; most stars work hard for many years before they make it. I sat next to him at a fight in Vegas right before he was getting ready to perform at the halftime show at the 2014 Super Bowl to be held at the MetLife Stadium in New Jersey. He said, "Damn, man. You know, I'm a local Hawaii boy. I can't believe I'm going to have to be out there in the cold like that. My voice may freeze." Bruno keeps it real, is down-to-earth, and is just one of the guys. He is generous and loves to talk about talented people he knows who are just coming up—like his sisters, who are forming a band that he will be behind all the way. Bruno is the full package. He cares about being righteous as a person along with being great as an artist. It's rare that I come across a talent who stops me in my tracks. Bruno Mars is one of them.

Eva Longoria is a storybook example of a star I've had the joy of watching come from nowhere to the top and not change in the least. I should probably state that we are the best of friends. A question I hear from fans all the time is "How come you've never gone out with Eva Longoria? You guys would be perfect together. You two could be the Latino Kennedys!"

That's a funny question, because I've known her for so many years now and the friendship has always been platonic. I met Eva when she first pulled into LA in her little Ford Escort, straight outta San Antonio. She and I are roughly the same age, we're both Mexican, and we share a similar understanding about the ways of the world. We just hit it off. Whether it was timing or the fact that I felt she was more like a sister than a potential love interest, we never pushed the romantic thing. That said, she was always a rock star to me—pretty, smart, passionate, and sexy. We've joked that she is my female equivalent: she has the same energy, drive, focus, and, best of all, the same sense of humor. We crack up together all the time.

As Eva grew in Hollywood stature, from aspiring actress to one of the leads of *Desperate Housewives* to producer and star to mover and shaker, she didn't change her values or her priorities— she's still the funny, cool woman I met with the little Ford hatchback. Eva cares about her culture and her community and has become such a strong voice in it; her activism makes me truly proud to call her a friend.

In the past, fans used to assume that when we appeared in pictures together—in a bunch of tabloids—we were, in fact, a couple. But that has never been the case. We used to call each other and laugh hysterically about the rumors we could make up. Let that be a lesson not to trust what you read in the tabloids. On occasion, we've worked together—including cohosting the ALMA Awards one year—and we are always looking for opportunities to do more together.

Indeed, hosting has helped me claim a platform for doing more to spur opportunity for Latinos in the entertainment industry and I have to credit Eva's leadership, as well as the support from others. Not just because we share a family name, but I happen to have a lot of respect for George Lopez and Jennifer Lopez, who are true leaders in the cause. J.Lo, a superstar on every level, and I work on NUVO, an English-language entertainment TV network for the modern American Latino. English speaking but with a Latin flair. There's a whole new generation out there and they want hip programming and media outlets.

George Lopez and I have worked together both on his show and on other projects. He's a great guy and fiercely talented as a comic. In the last season of *X Factor*, I was able to chaperone George's daughter on set and she is now my best friend—probably because she was able to get pictures taken with One Direction when they were on the show. Anything George or Jennifer asks me to do, I'll be there for them. And when I've asked them, they've been there for me.

Can we make a difference together in creating opportunities that continue to be closed to our peers from Latino backgrounds? Well, I absolutely believe we can.

If you were to ask me what I love most of all about being the host of *Extra* and about hosting in general, I would say that it's the chance to learn and grow every single day. That's why whenever I'm asked if I miss being in front of the camera as an actor—even though I don't rule out saying yes to acting or performing roles that come along—I point out that there's so much more I need to learn before I realize my ambition of being the Latino Dick Clark.

Recently I was asked if I'm ever tempted to pursue opportunities that take me out of my comfort zone, much like my role in *A Chorus Line*. The answer is that I'm always open to possibilities that will let me continue my journey in the entertainment world. But just how far out of my comfort zone I should go is a question to consider. When I was younger, I had the opportunity, for example, to take a shot in the music business as part of a boy band, complete with Auto-Tuning and dancing and megatours. But as exciting as that sounded, I turned it down because I happen to agree with Clint Eastwood, who once said, "A man's got to know his limitations." Diversity as a performer in show business has been unbelievably rewarding for me, but I also try to stay in my lane. Anyway, I sort of fulfilled living out the music thing by playing the drums back in the day. When the offers arose, my instincts told me to focus on my acting and not be distracted by musical ambitions. Some actors can move seamlessly into music, and some recording artists do well as actors. But those who can command respect in those different arenas tend to be few and far between.

Maybe I've seen too much from the big chair, but I know that sometimes you can undervalue what you have and reach out for something else, yet it's like reaching out for the trapeze bar and missing—only there's no net. Once you fall, you fall hard. And that's it.

All of that said, if I had to do it all over again knowing what I do now, I would have pushed myself out of my comfort zone even more and dared to reach for dreams that would have let me soar farther as a daring young man on a high-flying trapeze. Most of what held me back was worrying about what would happen if I failed and what this or that person would think of me. Would I have been fearless if I could do it again? No, I wouldn't be fearless. But I would try to fear less. Fear is the thing that keeps you from living true to who you really are. Advice to self: Fear not what others think of you. Fear not bad outcomes. Move forward in life with aplomb.

The fact is, I love what I do and where I am. My life is a dream come true—so amazing that I have to pinch myself frequently. But what I do isn't what makes me happy. My happiness has to do with the love that surrounds me, the people who love me, and those I love. They're the reason I do all of this.

Guess what. Those are the stories coming up next. I've saved the best for last.

# CHAPTER 8

# MAZZA

Not long before I left the cast of *A Chorus Line*, a new cast member—or so I thought—arrived just in time to change my life forever. Even though neither one of us had any clue of that when we first met.

Let me set the stage for that moment. Literally—as I happened to actually be standing backstage left, warming up before that evening's performance. As you may recall, this was the summer of 2008 and my run with the show was drawing to a close. By this point, my focus was on juggling not just my time on Broadway but also my crazy bicoastal hosting schedule with MTV's *ABDC* and with making inroads as a host on *Extra*—all-consuming.

At thirty-five years old, I finally felt I knew who I was and what I wanted—and it wasn't to hit the clubs and be in the scene. It had been a few weeks since the tragedy of losing my cousin and godson Chico, whose life had been so tough, and I'd been thinking about doing more to cherish the life in front of me. Down the road, I could see myself making space to share it with someone else—someone who shared values and interests with me, along with passion. In that reflective state, I was starting to think I was ready, maybe for the first time ever, for that kind of relationship. Something real and lasting.

Even so, that was not the priority. And that's why it wasn't a big deal in the middle of my stage left warm-up when I heard our stage manager say he wanted to introduce me to an actress who would be joining the cast as part of the ensemble—both in the chorus and on swing, doing several of the smaller roles, all of which entailed nonstop dancing, singing, and acting. As I finished stretching out my legs, I looked up and saw a strikingly beautiful woman standing in front of me—big brown eyes, long dark hair. She was curvy, athletic, with a dancer's body.

Just then a bell went off in my head. For a few weeks I'd been hearing about some girl who was going to be joining the show. According to fellow cast member Nick Adams, a gifted Broadway triple threat who played the role of my character's assistant in the show, "You're going to really like this new girl. She's just your type. Gorgeous, Italian, exotic. You're going to love her." But he hadn't mentioned a name.

As I smiled and stood to greet her, I figured this must be the girl Nick had mentioned. Hand outstretched and dimpled smile blazing, I said, "Nice to meet you. I'm Mario."

She reached out her hand to shake mine and said, matter-of-factly, "Hi, Mario, my name is Courtney."

Hmm. I thought if she was Italian she would have some exotic name like Francesca or Isabella.

So I said, "Courtney? That's it?"

"Yeah, that's it." She shrugged.

"Well, I thought you were going have some Italian name." I laughed, wondering if Nick had misinformed me. "You are Italian, right?"

Yes, she confirmed that she was, telling me her last name: "Mazza."

To which I replied, "Why Courtney?"

"What do you want from me? I was born in the eighties," she shot back.

Wow, she *was* sassy. She was also clearly not impressed by my poor attempt at engaging her in conversation and appeared to not really be paying attention to me at all. So, not able to think quickly enough of anything else, I went for small talk as I returned to my warm-up stretches, needing to sweat out some of the previous night's alcohol intake.

"Oh, man," I said, grinning. "I think I had a rougher night than I thought." She didn't say a word, other than to glance at me blankly, so I blundered on. "Yeah, I don't know how tonight's gonna be. Could be a rough one for me." Lame as that was, I had to break the ice somehow. All I could do was repeat that it was nice to meet her and to say, "Welcome aboard."

I knew Courtney Mazza had to have a real edge when she looked up at me, raised an eyebrow, and correctively said, "Oh, I've been on this show before. You didn't know? You're the one who should get the 'welcome aboard.'" And then she walked away without looking back.

Oh, snap!

Yep, before I arrived Courtney had apparently been in this production but had left to do another show called *Cry-Baby*. And now that she was back, I didn't have much time to win her over.

Why I was so intrigued, I don't know exactly. There was something about her. Watching her in the show, I was definitely impressed. Only in her midtwenties, she was wildly talented and did it all—dancing, singing, and making different characters come to life with the acting chops of a true pro.

As the days passed, I continued to try to talk to her. I'd try chitchat or idle banter or being sweet and thoughtful or newsworthy—just anything to hit on a topic of conversation that would engage her. She was cool and didn't act like she minded so much, as her focus wasn't on me. But I pressed on, attempting not to be so obvious as to be a total loser.

To be honest, I began to suspect that she was ignoring me on purpose. My ego wouldn't let me believe she didn't like me, so I convinced myself that her snarky attitude was only a ploy—that the whole "I'm not interested in you" was part of her strategy for winning the hearts of men. After all, when she turned me down for going out for a cup of coffee, she literally said she was not interested in me. Ploy or genuine disinterest, it didn't matter. But her aloof attitude worked, because I became even more intrigued. On the few occasions when I managed to grab her attention and talk to her, she was always very quick-witted.

Like, one day I arrived at the theater feeling very jet-lagged and passed her as we headed toward the dressing rooms. "Oh, man," I said. "I'm feeling kind of rough today."

"Don't worry. I'm not checking you out." Delivered with a twinkle in her eye, and total deadpan.

Courtney was killing me. I couldn't believe that, on top of all the other things I liked about her, she was funny too. If a girl is funny, to me that's incredibly sexy. Usually I end up being the comedian in a relationship. Not that we had a relationship, but I was loving that she was smart and quick and funny and sassy—the four food groups of a perfect woman.

One afternoon as a group of us were leaving the theater after a matinee, I happened to be walking next to her and, being myself, I teasingly said, "You know what? Courtney is not working for me. You need a name that matches you—you know, Italian, exotic." Since I called most of my friends by their last names or gave them nicknames, I told her, "How 'bout I call you by your last name? I'm going to call you Mazza."

"Screw you," she said, but with a laugh. "Just so you know, I don't like Mario."

Zing!

Well, you know what they say in comedy: if it works once, you milk it until you can't anymore. The next time I sidled up to her, I told her, of course, Courtney was a beautiful name, but not like a name that rolled easily off the tongue—like maybe it was too Caucasian. She shook her head and tried to refrain from smiling. Not that I was even thinking about falling in love or having a real relationship at that point, but if we were ever going to get past "No, I'm not interested," I actually had trouble seeing myself dating a Courtney. But Mazza worked for me and, lo and behold, she laughed at her new nickname.

Progress! We had advanced to joking around. And if I had any reservations about my interest in her, as soon as she made me laugh, I was hooked. She owned me. But there was that minor detail that she wouldn't go out with me. I asked her out so often that that too became a running joke. Every day at work, I'd say, "Come on, when are you going to go out with me?" She had a boyfriend; of course she did. Why wouldn't she? She was incredible.

I enlisted Nick, who knew her outside of the show, to get the scoop on Mazza and find out more and whether there was any hope to get her to go out with me. Ah, the irony. The same Nick who played my assistant in the show, and who first told me about her, was now tasked with assisting me in cracking the code to get a date with Mazza. So he had to help! Next thing I knew, we were in the midst of a Shakespearean comedy of errors—or a plot from an old *Saved by the Bell*—with Nick as the go-between and all kinds of strategies backfiring on me. Each time Nick told her I wanted to go out, she wouldn't budge. He did find out that she had been with the same boyfriend for years—maybe ten years—and as I understood it, their relationship had probably become more habit than love.

I kept chipping away at the Mazza stone. I don't know if she and her boyfriend had a fight or whatever, but finally she succumbed. I like to think it was my charm and devilish good looks, but it was probably my pressure—a pressure that bordered on stalking. Not quite, of course, but still, that kind of campaigning is no way to get a date. However, it may have just been what got her to say yes to going out with me.

You would think that I would have cleared my calendar on the day we planned to get together, but I had a business meeting just before Courtney Mazza and I had arranged to meet. It wasn't just any meeting: I was to be sitting down with Katie Couric. Katie and I were laughing and having a great time, and I lost track of the hour. When I realized the time, I excused myself and called Mazza.

"I am so sorry—I can't get out of this meeting. Please forgive me—I'm going to be a little bit late for our date."

"Forget it," she said. She blew me off.

I emphatically apologized and then, after a week or so, she cooled off and agreed to give me another shot. This time I was early. I was waiting for her. As she approached, she looked incredible, but I could also see she wasn't alone. She'd brought Nick. He is gay, so he'd be no competition on our first date night. Smart move. I wasn't planning on making any moves or anything, so we all went out and had a good time, all three of us.

The more I got to know Mazza, the more I liked her. After our first date, she finally let her guard down a little bit. We started to hang out more and more. But she was also dealing with the dissolution of the long-term relationship she'd been in. And for my part, at this point I had only five weeks or so before I had to leave New York for LA for good.

The last thing I wanted with Courtney Mazza was to begin something and then try to maintain a long-distance relationship after I left. I'd been down that road and I knew it wouldn't work. Instead, I chose to live in the moment and just enjoy this really wonderful girl's company. We decided we were going to have fun as long as she wanted to hang out, and then we'd go our separate ways.

We'd grab a bite here, go for drinks after our show there, spend our day off at a museum or get takeout and stay at my place, where we seemed to find lots to do to entertain each other. Pretty soon we were together every day and I felt so comfortable that I gave her a key to my Times Square condo. When I gave it to her, I almost admitted that she already had the key to my heart. But I didn't want to spoil the simplicity of what we had.

As the time came closer for me to leave, I could only feel thankful for what a nice, wholesome time she and I had shared, so different from the first part of the run, when I was partying and going out and feeling a bit lost and lonely. How lucky I was to have met Mazza and that, thanks to Nick as well as to my own persistence, we had gotten to connect in such a deep, real way. The fact that it was going to end when I returned to LA—and we both knew it—couldn't dampen the precious time we spent together. Romantic though I am, I had enough life experience at this stage to know the difference between what is meant to be forever and what is futile. I wasn't going to delude myself into thinking our time together could be a forever thing.

Logistics alone made anything else unfeasible. After my six-month run was up, I had to get back to Los Angeles. And after Mazza had fulfilled her commitment to *A Chorus Line*, she would go right into another show on Broadway. Wow. She was going from one show to another, three shows back to back to back. When it was time to say good-bye, we didn't get overly dramatic; we just wished each other well. Mazza wasn't necessarily thrilled about her new gig, though, because it was Disney's *The Little Mermaid* and I think she wanted something a bit more edgy. Still, that was a coup for anyone and I reminded her, "Are you kidding me? This is what you've worked for all your life—you're on Broadway working at the top of the field." No, it wasn't Shakespeare, but . . . my God! I went on, "There are people who would give anything to be working like you."

Mazza just smiled at me and looked down. She was too talented not to stay busy with work and I knew she was going to be just fine without me. She'd probably forget about me in a week or so.

Work consumed me when I went back to LA and for the first few weeks my life picked up its pace and everything rushed forward as usual. Except, no, something was missing. I missed Mazza. This can't be, I thought. We would talk on the phone and keep in touch, but we never discussed or intimated wanting anything more from each other. Neither of us mentioned flying to see the other. Yet I wanted to see her face, not just hear her voice. But I had every intention of adhering to my rule: no long-distance relationships.

Skype saved this relationship because, when we were video chatting, it was almost like we were together in the same room. It was great to be able to look into her eyes from so far away. She began to admit that she was missing me a lot too, and so the longing for each other began. I didn't want to miss her because I knew succumbing to the romantic melancholy of being in love with someone far away was impractical. She lived in New York. I lived in LA. You can't get much farther apart in the States. She might as well have lived in Outer Mongolia. Even if she lived just a state away, it would have been complicated.

Our Skype video chats weren't enough after a while, however. Before long I couldn't handle wanting to be with her in person. So I finally asked, "Hey, why don't you come out and visit me on your day off? I'll get you a ticket. Come on. I know it's a quick turn-around, but I miss you. It'd be great to see you."

Yes, it was extremely romantic and passionate and wonderful and exciting and didn't make any sense at all. On paper it was stupid, but in our hearts it was perfection. She flew all the way out and was literally here for twenty-four hours, not even two nights.

Rinse and repeat. We became hooked on each other and it got to the point where she was coming to visit me almost every other week. Something magical does happen when you only have so much time to be together. Making the most of every minute, we were in my bed when I first told her I loved her. It felt really right, even though the logistics were so wrong. Love may not conquer all, but when a man falls in love, he's conquered. Seeing each other in person once every week or so didn't make up for how much I continued to miss her the rest of the time.

And then it happened. Mazza came to a crossroads with the show she was in. It wasn't as gratifying as she had hoped, for various reasons, and she was unhappy. She was going to quit.

"Why do you want to quit?" I asked. "Working actresses should keep working. You're still on Broadway—starring on Broadway. It's awesome! Why would you want to quit?" That was the input I would have given to myself or anyone I loved.

"I just need a break." Her plan was to leave the show at the beginning of the summer and take the summer off.

My wheels began spinning with possible scenarios. It wasn't

as if we could go on and on with this flying back and forth once every other week. It was taxing and not fair to either of us. Damn. I had promised myself I wouldn't be foolish enough to get into a long-distance relationship, and somehow I found myself smack in the middle of one. I asked Mazza, "Well, if you're going to take a break, can I convince you to come take a break and spend time here in LA? Let me take care of your apartment expenses back in New York for three months so you don't have to worry about it. You'll come out here and we'll spend the summer together. By the end of the summer, we'll know if, you know, this is really serious. You may not be able to stand me after a week! And no harm, no foul—your apartment's already taken care of and you're going to take a break anyway, so you're not missing out on anything."

There was a brief silence on the other end of the phone. But finally she agreed to take me up on the offer to come out and give us a try.

Looking back on that summer, I remember that everything flowed like a dance, as if we were moving in sync to a rhythm that filled our days with laughter and the little things of life that make it sweet. I remember her picking up on my quirks and starting to tease me.

"What are you doing?" She laughed at the movies when I opened my pack of Twizzlers and put it under my nose. So I like to smell everything before I eat it. So what?

I've done that since I was a kid. She thought it was hilarious and mocked me for it from then on. But that to me was a sign. Those are the little quirks that only someone who really gets you happens to notice. That is the stuff of love.

One of the best times of that summer was introducing her to my parents. Everybody loved her! Of course, I introduced her as Courtney, but before long my family started calling her Mazza too.

In my life, I had made some of my biggest mistakes by not following my instincts. This time I needed to listen. You know how sometimes when you're in a relationship there is some getting used to each other and it feels a little awkward at first and there are adjustments and all that? There was none of that in this relationship. It felt like we had been going out for years. It was so comfortable from day one, from the beginning. Being with her felt so natural, so right. The summer flew by and at the end of the three months I said, "I don't want you to go."

And Mazza said, "Well, I don't really want to go either."

And I said, "I can't go to New York. Can you stay here?"

She looked up at me, softly smiled—the kind of smile where you don't show your teeth—and said, "Yeah, I'll stay here with you, Mario. Why not?"

She had to give up her apartment in New York, and for anyone who's ever lived in that city, you know that giving up a coveted apartment is a scary prospect because finding a new one is beyond difficult. I alleviated her worries by saying, "If for some reason things don't work out, I'll find you another apartment and I'll take care of it and get you started again."

I also did not want her to give up her career for me or move to LA for me—this had to be her decision entirely. I had to be one hundred percent certain that this was what she wanted. I wanted her to be at a point where she was ready to make a change, to take the risk, but I didn't want to feel like I was coercing her into it. I wanted her to be at peace with walking away from her life in New York City and not regretfully thinking, "Why did I come? I shouldn't have given up my Broadway career. There's still stuff I long to do professionally."

I'm a performer and I know that everyone in my field has a list of things or benchmarks they want to achieve before they get out of the business. I couldn't live with the idea of convincing her to walk away from all that if she wasn't one hundred percent in. And I would feel guilty if she regretted her choice.

It just so happened that the timing was perfect for her to make the transition and for us to spend some quality time together in California. She had worked consistently and gone from show to show to show over many years. She had lived her dream of being a successful singer, dancer, and actress on Broadway. She had nice runs on big shows and was certainly accomplished in her profession. She didn't have a "Been there, done that" attitude, but I think she was comfortable with the idea of some downtime and was happy to spend time on growing our relationship.

The timing was right for both of us. Again, it's not always just about finding a great person with whom you can connect on a spiritual, sexual, and emotional level; it's about the great person coming into your life at just the right time. It did seem that the planets had aligned at the right time for Courtney Mazza and me. She stayed true to the plan and chose not to get an agent and start working out here. She could have easily pursued jobs in film and TV and landed roles, although she was looking forward to growth as a person in other ways. I thought maybe she would get antsy after a few months, but she didn't and we merged our lives seamlessly.

I wasn't scared, nor did I have any apprehensions about committing to Mazza. The only aftershock of what happened with my first marriage was that I was reluctant to get married too quickly. My thought was that I didn't need to get married to be happy. While that was in conflict with my Catholic beliefs, I believed that I personally could be happy with someone and even have a family without having a matrimonial contract. After all, doesn't commitment happen in the heart more than it does by signing on the dotted line?

Whether I could argue these points well or not, I knew that I wouldn't be getting married right away; I wanted to fully and soberly explore our new relationship. I just thought we could be happy together. She could be my companion, my partner; I could be hers. That was the plan and her decision to take me up on my offer to stay in Los Angeles worked out like a fairy tale. The relationship kept growing and our bond tightened as the days and weeks and months passed. My "little mermaid" and I have more or less lived happily ever after—from that day on.

A re the best things in life always planned? Sometimes. Can amazing things happen when you least expect them? Without a shadow of a doubt. In fact, the story of one of the most amazing blessings in my and Mazza's life is the proof.

I should mention that during the early months of setting up house together Mazza and I were in no hurry to try to start a family or rush anything along. We were head over heels—absolutely—but we were just settling in and wanted to enjoy each other. Then again, as we both had agreed, if it did happen we would be thrilled. None of these conversations changed my stance on getting married. We had a great thing with each other, true love by all accounts. I still didn't feel I needed to get married to prove to anyone that my love for Mazza was solid. Why mix it up if it was already a happy situation? Would that change if we found ourselves expecting a child? Not as far as I was concerned.

As it happened, I had been having some lengthy discussions with a friend of mine who was trying to get pregnant. It was extremely difficult for her. She had tried just about everything, but, unfortunately for her, nothing seemed to be working out. She's Hispanic too, which surprised the hell outta me—I'd always thought if you stared at a Latina long enough, she'd get pregnant. I'd never heard of a Mexican woman not being fertile.

Obviously, I was clueless about the issue of infertility. Not having been around that particular block, I had thought my whole life that women could easily get pregnant and we must take the necessary precautions if we don't want that to happen. My friend confided in me, sharing all the trials and tribulations she had gone through in her effort to get pregnant. I listened intently as she educated me on this technique or that medicine, this procedure or that method. As I learned about the intricacies of many ob-gyn concerns, I would often get Mazza's opinion and ask her what she thought.

I didn't get into too many specific details, out of respect for my friend's privacy, but I did say to Mazza, "My friend is struggling to get pregnant and spending a lot of money, and it's stressing her out and kind of depressing her." I didn't think it would be so difficult for my friend, who was young. But the reality for her and her husband at the time was worrisome—besides the cost of the fertility specialist, the need to get pregnant can monopolize every waking hour of your thought process and put a strain on the relationship if it's not handled properly.

After hearing about all this, Courtney and I started to think about our lack of hurry on getting pregnant and wondered if we could have this same problem. Up until now, we had never considered infertility a possibility; it was the furthest thing from our minds. Mazza and I had just passively begun talking about a family someday. You know, you get into those conversations about how you both want kids, you don't want kids, you want kids but only two, you want kids but they better be cute and not brats. We both agreed that we would like to build a family together someday. And we also decided that it didn't need to be anytime soon.

We talked more about my friend struggling and I told Mazza that my friend said, "If you're ever interested, you should meet with my doctor and he can check out Courtney just to be on the safe side—you know, just in case, whatever. It's best you find out now if there is anything you have to do or if there are any preventative measures you may need to take."

Mazza agreed it was a good idea and set up an appointment. She was going to get checked out anyway, but she didn't yet have a gynecologist in Los Angeles that she trusted. This just seemed like a proactive thing to do and we were both grateful for a positive referral from my friend.

When Mazza returned from this appointment, her face was ashen as she met me at the door. Nothing whatsoever could have prepared me for the news that what they discovered was heart-wrenching and alarming.

She had tumors and cysts on her ovaries. According to the doctors, the way things were inside, she would never be able to get pregnant. We were both in shock. Here we were feeling bad for my friend, only to find out we were in dire circumstances ourselves. We could have tried and failed for years and never known why if Courtney hadn't done her impromptu checkup. The truth is, despite our lack of hurry to get pregnant, we had quietly been trying to have a baby. We didn't tell a soul because we wanted it to be a surprise.

After Mazza told me the worst of the news, we took a few minutes to acknowledge our shock and worry. Then I asked, "What did they suggest we do?"

"Well, they suggest surgery right away." But even then, they couldn't guarantee anything; because of the scar tissue that would result from such invasive surgery, she could go through the operation to remove the cysts but still not ever be able to have kids.

A major, major blow to both of us. That was a tough time for us, but as any strong couple knows, these are the moments in life that can take a relationship to the next level and strengthen the bond. That's exactly what our crisis did.

My thoughts were mainly focused on Courtney's health and well-being. I was trying not to be selfish and think of the dreams of a family that could be shattered. It was just unbelievable news, like being smashed in the gut with an unseen uppercut. I felt dizzy and my face was going flush. My head swam with many different thoughts all at once. All I could do was tell Mazza, "I love you, and we'll get through this together."

Mazza quietly explained that the doctor advised getting the tumors out of there no matter what. It looked fairly safe if they did it right away. Imagine if she had not gone for that checkup, or if she'd gone to the doctor later on—it would have been worse. The odds would have been even slimmer for the love of my life to be healthy again.

As much as I tried to keep a stiff upper lip for Mazza, I became really sad and needed to spend time by myself to deliberate. In the process, I sank into a fleeting state of depression. Finally I said, "Let's get the surgery right away."

The ordeal actually seemed to worsen when we met with the doctor and were given a range of outcomes that focused on the worst-case scenario. "We don't know, we don't know, we don't know" was all we heard from them. I felt really helpless in that moment. I wanted to say, "We're paying you because that medical degree on your wall is saying that you *do know*."

Mazza had the surgery as the doctor suggested, and then we just had to wait. She was the best patient she could be, and recovered quickly from surgery. But the last thing I felt was patient. Yet all we could do was wait for recovery and wait to see if she would ever get pregnant. The doctors replayed their broken record: "We don't know what's going to happen."

Mazza and I decided we would let nature take its course. We assumed the odds were astronomically low that we had any chance of bringing life into this world, but we never lost hope. The way the doctor painted the picture, we should know that the time would come to think about adoption or other options.

We were grateful, though, that she had come through the surgery without any of the worst-case outcomes and that she was otherwise healthy. Within no time, Mazza was back to her high-energy, passion-filled self, and within a couple of weeks we were able to resume our love life as before. We had so much to be thankful for.

And then, a short time later, I came home from a hike to receive shocking, life-altering news. When Mazza heard me come in, she yelled from the top of the stairs, "I'm pregnant!"

I stood there paralyzed. Had she just told me she was pregnant? If that was the case, boy, I guessed that pregnancy announcements sure didn't happen the way they do in the movies. Nope. Courtney Mazza had just made this earth-shattering announcement with no more of a grandiose delivery than if she'd yelled, "Hey, your mother called."

My head began to spin. Was this a trick? Just to be sure it wasn't, I yelled back up the stairs, "What?"

"I'm pregnant!"

Then I had to sit down to steady myself. I even remember what I was wearing and I'm sure it will be etched into my mind forever: red shorts, sneakers, and a black headband on my head. At long last the news registered and I stood up. "Whoa, really? That's awesome! Oh my God, come here—I want to hug you right now."

And she did! We hugged and hugged and wept happy tears.

This was a miracle, in defiance of the odds. As it turned out, only three short weeks after the surgery—*bam*—Mazza had gotten pregnant, at a time when we weren't even trying! Mazza is obviously as tough as a marine and apparently I've got some Michael Phelps–swimming sperm.

Nine months later—actually closer to ten months, which I know because of the expertise I've gained—our miracle arrived in person. Not exactly planned, but also no accident. More like divine intervention and now we've got this little blessing of a little girl we thought we'd never be able to have.

Isn't that amazing? Miraculous but true.

Soon after Mazza got pregnant a friend of mine approached me and asked if we would be interested in doing a reality show documenting becoming first-time parents. I wasn't sure I wanted to share this special time in our lives with cameras following us around, but I thought it was interesting enough to discuss with the mom-to-be.

And she said, "Well, maybe it could be fun. We can document the entire experience for later on in life. Imagine if you and I had a well-produced documentary of our own births?"

We both decided it would be like a bunch of home videos. We'll do it just up until when the baby is born. I said, "Okay, let's do it. I don't want to pitch it or anything, but if somebody's interested or whatever, with no stress and strife, we'll do it."

My friend Chris Abrego has a great working relationship with VH1 and in one phone call to the network we had a show. We didn't have to do a test pilot. But it may have been the wrong network for us. For one, Mazza and I are not dramatic. We're not drunk, pulling each other's hair and running around the house naked chasing each other. I wanted to capture something positive, fun, and funny. I thought the premise was a guy who didn't expect to be a dad. Ultimately, I thought the show would be cool home videos to show our baby when she grew up and they would have incredible production quality. It wasn't that bad for me having a film crew around during the nine-month pregnancy and it wasn't difficult for Mazza—she's a natural entertainer and performer, and she's goofy. The production teams working on our show weren't invasive and all in all it was a wonderful experience.

It was a great piece of documenting. I'm proud of the way it turned out. The people who saw it loved it. They certainly got their drama at the end because it was very dramatic when I almost missed the birth. I was working as a host for a fight in Vegas—three weeks before the due date—and got the call that Courtney could possibly be going into labor and was being rushed to the hospital. Not wasting a second, I jumped on the last flight out of Vegas and flew back to LA, racing straight to the hospital, where I found Mazza being prepped for an emergency C-section, because she had something called placenta previa.

Fifteen minutes later, we had a little girl!

We had made a solemn oath, Mazza and I, that we wouldn't know the sex of the baby in advance. Like a broken record, I had begged her, "Mazza, you have to promise that we won't peek at the sex of our child. No matter how tempting. Let's wait to find out. It'll be the best surprise ever."

So we went old school and kept our baby's sex a secret. My theory was that if God wanted you to know ahead of time, he would have put a window in a woman's stomach.

I walked out of the emergency room that night to greet my friends who were also awaiting the news for a variety of reasons: not only were they supportive, we also all had bets on the gender and the weight of the baby—we'd taken a *baby pool*. Everyone who'd put in a bet had to guess the gender and the weight. It got up to over twelve hundred dollars. I rushed out and yelled, "It's a girl!" When the cheering stopped, they all asked, "How much? How much does she weigh?"

My buddy Tuddy won. Tuddy, whose real name is Rod, is always dressed with a certain style that looks like he could step onto the set of *Goodfellas*—hence his nickname. Also, because he's just that cool. We decided we would use *Price Is Right* rules, and I was one ounce higher than Tuddy. Tuddy won by betting eight pounds, eleven ounces, right on the money.

My sister, Marissa, picked the name. I initially wanted the name Francesca because I wanted to be able to call her Frankie. I just thought a little girl named Frankie Lopez would be really cool. However, Mazza has a niece named Francesca, so she didn't want to add another relative with the same name.

"So what?" I complained. "The other Francesca lives in Chicago—how confusing will that be? It won't."

Mazza argued with me—and she puts a lot of passion behind her point of view, I'll tell you that—so the compromise was that we kept Francesca as a middle name. We wanted a nice Italian name because my wife is one hundred percent Italian. Obviously, Lopez covers the Spanish part. We thought maybe Sofia or Lucia would make good first names. You know the drill—everyone in the family helps deliberate over what you should call your kid. Hell, they have entire books written with name options. I thought Sofia Lopez had a nice ring to it. I liked the idea of her having a pretty name and at the same time a cool name. I also liked Lucia Lopez, but worried it sounded a bit too much like a fighter. "In this corner, weighing in at eight pounds, eleven ounces, is Lucia Lopez." It was my sister who mentioned the name Gia. "I've always liked the name Gia," she said.

And I said, "Yeah, you know what? That is a great name." I

said it out loud to see how it felt: "Gia Francesca Lopez." It sounded like a beautiful cruise ship. "Sailing aboard the *Gia Francesca* . . ." I thought Gia Francesca Lopez had a beautiful ring to it. Very Italian and Hispanic, a name that captured both our backgrounds.

After Gia was born, we had a bit of a scare because the nurse thought something was physically wrong with our little girl. Ironically, some of the nurses and doctors who deliver babies don't necessarily know much about babies other than the procedure of delivering them. They are trained to do various assessment tests to recognize development concerns, and the possibility that there was something wrong—that is, a disability—was raised. The nurse was speculating and we were bombarded with a deluge of complicated information and surreal possibilities. They had to run a bunch of tests. For two weeks, our life was hell because of an inconclusive speculation by one of the nurses. I know she was just doing her job, but I wish they had a way to do it without making the parents paranoid and scared. She was doing her due diligence, but it was the most stressful two weeks of my life.

Gia Francesca Lopez did not have any disability—not that we would have adored her any less. Actually, my daughter has advanced physical and verbal skills—my God, you can't shut her up. She's beautiful, super smart, a good little girl. As healthy as can be.

Not surprisingly, she is hilarious and loves to perform. She is really an angel, our firstborn, our Gia Francesca—one of my biggest blessings to date.

So much joy and gratitude flowed in our home after Gia's birth. But the Catholic guilt started to hang over my head—that nagging voice in my head telling me I needed to be married. Besides, I wanted us all to have the same last name. This reached a head when

Mazza told me that she went to go fill one of Gia's prescriptions and the pharmacist was holding up the process because Courtney Mazza had a different last name than Gia, whose legal name is Gia Francesca Lopez. We had to do something about this, and quick.

She called me and said, "You know, it kind of made me sad that I had to prove that I was her mom because I had a different last name than our little girl. I had to show my ID but they kept hassling me."

My immediate thought was that I too wanted us all to have the same last name. We're a family and I wanted something tangible to show that we belong together. I loved Mazza, our beautiful daughter, and the life we were building together. But first I had to take myself through the paces.

What was holding me back? Nothing. It was high time that Mazza and I let go of the boyfriend/girlfriend labels and repackage ourselves into husband and wife. She was the mother of my child and I wanted her to be my wife. It was time to tie the knot. I made up my mind that very moment that I wanted to marry her.

Instead of proposing right away, I started talking about it generally without making it official. The truth is, I had known she was the one for me since almost the day I met her. Without saying the M-word (marriage) just yet, we also began to talk about having another kid sooner rather than later. We knew how hard it was and that nothing was guaranteed. According to the opinions of several doctors, just because we'd successfully had Gia didn't mean we could easily conceive another. We both agreed that if we were going to get married in a ceremony, speaking hypothetically, we didn't want a pregnant Mazza walking down the aisle.

The hypotheticals ended during our Christmas vacation following Gia's birth, when we traveled for the holidays down to Zihuatanejo, Mexico. Remember the final scene in *The Shawshank*

*Redemption*, where Andy describes his little place on the beach? That was the paradise location I had chosen to finally pop the question. We went for a walk together along the sand. Holding hands, just being quiet together. The sky was blue, the sun shone brightly, and out of nowhere a group of mariachis playing the music of my youth came strolling up, singing and playing as I got down on my knees and asked the question: "Courtney Mazza, will you be my wife?"

And as I think you know now, she said yes.

Exactly one year later, on December 18, 2012, we became husband and wife in an incredible winter wedding in Mexico at Casa Aramara. My close friend Michael Schultz, or Schultzy as I like to call him, arranged everything and it was absolutely stunning. Both the ceremony and the reception were held outdoors and the heat was intense. During the emotional ceremony, I couldn't help glancing over at my parents, who, this time, had big, wide smiles on their faces as they let the tears flow freely. The wedding began around three in the afternoon and went until the wee hours of the morning. Everyone had the time of their lives sweating it out on the massive dance floor we had set up. The tequila and the muggy Mexican night began to take their toll and slowly but surely a tie came off, suit coats were tossed on chairs, men rolled up their sleeves; then a pair of shoes got kicked off, women put their hair up, and before you knew it, everyone in the wedding party had jumped in the pool. Including my good friend Eva Longoria. Weddings can be stressful, but ours was one big party and everyone had a great time. Both Mrs. Lopez and I could not have been happier.

In the midst of planning the wedding festivities, we decided we should get going again on trying to have another child. We breathed a huge sigh of relief when we conceived right away. But a short time later, Mazza and I went on another roller-coaster ride when that pregnancy ended in a miscarriage. All kinds of worries and sadness set in, but we were assured by others that having a miscarriage is much more common than we knew.

We sat down together on the couch, I held her hand, we looked at each other, and I said, "Let's not stress about this. I'm glad you're okay and healthy. Let's leave it in God's hands." I believed that when the time was right Mazza would get pregnant again. We put our focus on Gia and on our happy family of three.

As time passed and Mazza and I didn't get pregnant, we again began to think, well, maybe we should talk to doctors; maybe we should see whether something is wrong. All sorts of thoughts swam in our heads: maybe we just got lucky with Gia; maybe we should try fertility treatments or something that would better our chances of having another baby. As soon as we started to explore those options—but before doing any of them—we ended up getting pregnant.

Maybe all Mazza really needed was a wedding ring. As it turned out, our second child was due almost exactly nine months after we were married!

During the pregnancy, we went through multiple rounds of different name suggestions for our baby on the way, with options for boy names and girl names. Of course, I thought about how cool it would be to have a boy. I'd grown up in a family with one boy and one girl and we were such a close family unit, I loved that possibility. But either way, I was just as excited as the first time.

In the event that we did have a boy, I was adamant that he wasn't going to be circumcised. First of all, in our modern times it's unnecessary and barbaric, in my opinion. If you're Jewish and/or it's part of a traditional religious rite, that's different. But there is no reason for the medical establishment to promote a procedure that is traumatic. We're not living in a time when a person bathes once every couple of weeks, creating a toxic environment where a man could be prone to infection in that part of his anatomy. No doctor that I've asked believes that circumcision is necessary in our day and age.

The second reason I felt so strongly was that I'm not circumcised and, frankly, I think it would be confusing to a son. My wife didn't argue with me about it because, clearly, she could tell how passionate I am about this issue. In a marriage, you have to pick your battles carefully. Here's a funny little secret for you: Mazza had never seen an uncircumcised penis before she saw mine—she was intrigued, fascinated, all of the above. Another secret, if you don't know, is that when an uncircumcised penis becomes erect, it looks the same as every other penis.

My point is, I'm how God made me, and so are all the men from my family and my neighborhood and in our culture. And by the way, you go anywhere in the world outside of this country and most men are like me—not circumcised.

So that was a nonissue as we awaited the baby's due date. In searching for a potential name for a boy, we followed the same guidelines we had when naming Gia. The name had to be a Spanish/Italian combination. Mario is an Italian name, but I didn't want to have a junior—and I'm not a junior, even though people assume that I am because my first and last names are the same as Dad's. But because I lack the middle name, I'm not a real junior and prefer not to be called one. None of my Jewish friends are juniors; they tell me that the tradition in their culture is to name babies in honor of family members no longer alive or just with the initials of loved ones. If we weren't going to use Mario, I really liked my grandfather's name, Luciano, which is also Italian. We considered that, but as

Mazza was very close to her late grandfather Domenico, a very Italian name, that got our attention. That's the sort of name you see on the side of a jar of spaghetti sauce. Maybe it sounded a little *too* Italian. So I said, "Let's compromise and go with the name Dominic." Mazza's family used to call her grandfather Nico, which I liked. I've always liked the name Dominic because it just so happens all the Dominics I've ever known were decent guys. Plus, Dominic Lopez sounds cool. Right? Even his initials are cool. "I'm keeping it on the *D.L.*" We decided not to give him a middle name. Dominic gets no middle name because I didn't get a middle name. Tradition!

You're probably wondering, in case you don't already know, if all this planning for a boy was for naught? Well, sure enough, at long last Dominic Lopez, our son, burst into this life to great celebration and fanfare from his doting parents and three-year-old big sister and grandparents, aunts, uncles, cousins on all the sides of the family. Kids are the miracles of our lives, I truly believe. They make us strive more—to provide, protect, teach, and love them.

From the moment he got here, Nico has made us laugh. I can't wait until he's big enough to learn to wrestle. There's so much I want to teach him, I'm going to have to start making notes. Of course, I want to teach him to work hard and be a gentleman when he starts showing an interest in girls and to remember that faith and family are there to support him all the way. I have also thought about the fact that when Dominic is only twenty years old, I'm going to be sixty. But I'm going to be a badass sixty and intend to be looking good and having the energy to keep up with him. I'll probably still be able to kick his ass if he wants to go a few rounds in the ring. I hope I can. By the time he hits thirty or so, though, he just might be able to whup me.

Courtney and I hit the jackpot with each other and with our

two extraordinary children. I want them to have incredible, fulfilling lives—all the good that I had, and some of the experiences that I missed.

They're already blessed with two parents who really love, support, and show them—with real actions—how we both feel about them. How would I do things a little differently as a father than my dad did? I love Dad very much, but one thing I will do differently is verbalize my feelings more, especially in telling Gia and Dominic that I love them. My father, who I love and who I know loves me, is a very old-school, macho tough guy, and he has never said the words "I love you, Mario."

Again, I know he loves me more than anything. I'm not trying to be sappy, but he's just never said those words to me. Does that hurt my feelings? No, because I get it. I know how he is and that he tells me in other ways that he loves me. However, because I think my kids will like hearing it as much as I love saying it, I tell my kids I love them every single day. Three and four times a day sometimes. You can't love your kids too much. You can't say "I love you" enough to the people who matter.

I want my kids to be as well-rounded as possible. Courtney and I will expose them to as many different things as we can the way my mother did for me: the arts, theater, dance, sports, and travel.

Most important, I want to raise good, quality individuals. People who will benefit society and not be part of the burden that already exist. I want my kids to be respectful, good people, to care about others, to be polite, hard workers, not take anything for granted, know the value of a dollar, and be able to depend on themselves, not anyone else. I know this is a tall list to fill and I know it will require an immense amount of energy from Mazza and myself. The good news is that we have so many like-minded friends and relatives that I'm confident we will raise our kids with a "village worth" of support—and I do believe it takes a village to raise a child.

If everything keeps going well for me, my children should be financially set, but I want them to have a sense of doing for themselves. My kids are going to have responsibilities and they're going to have jobs, whether it starts with jobs around the house or jobs I can help them find in my line of work. They're not going to get a free ride! Remember, I'm still the son of Richard and Elvia Lopez, and laziness will certainly be discouraged.

After Dominic arrived, we celebrated as only our Mexican and Italian families know how to do: with lots of excuses to get together, naturally.

We don't do traditional baby showers; we do what we call the Sip and See, which is nothing like a baby shower. In a Sip and See, you come, you have drinks, you sip, and you see the baby. It's more of a party atmosphere. And instead of asking for gifts, we ask for donations to a charity. Both Mazza and I are all set and there are many people in the world who don't have their basic necessities met. We like to use events like our wedding or the birth of our kids to give back to people who truly need a little help—as well as getting a chance for Gia and Nico to grow up surrounded by all the relatives.

Mazza and I try to celebrate the little moments with our kids too. There is nothing better than when I wake up in the morning to the sound of six-month-old Dominic babbling or when I hear Gia's little feet running down the steps and her voice calling, "Daddy! Daddy! Wake up!" Oh, and to see those big smiles and how they're so full of life and energy. It just melts my heart. You can't help but be in a good mood. And when they hug you, when they look you in the eye and say, "I love you, Daddy," I'd do anything.

It's just unbelievable. And I don't take any of it for granted. I can't imagine life BC—before children. Where would I be without the posse that awaits me when I walk through the front door at the end of the day and hear my daughter say, "Daddy's home!" She runs to me and jumps in my arms as Mazza, Nico in her arms, hurries in for our group hug. Then no matter what kind of day I've had, no matter what stress I've gone through, no matter what's happened, it makes it all better when I have all those arms wrapped around me. That makes it all worth it. That's why I want to work hard, stay focused, and do the right thing for my kids, for my family. And that's why I pray to be able to be the best husband, best father, best provider, and best me that I can be.

So how does the balancing act happen on a daily basis? Being the face of entertainment news is a weighty role to play and, not surprisingly, the pace can be pretty hectic. You know by now that I've never shied away from hard work or sleep deprivation when it's part of the job description. But with my young family at home, I try harder than ever to stay balanced. Depending on whether I'm going out for a run or not, I wake up around six, give or take, and have breakfast with my family, always, because they're the most important part of my life and I usually don't see them until the end of the day. Mazza and I put Dominic on the kitchen island on a blanket or in his little cradle thing so he can be with us as we eat. He'll stare at us like we're aliens and sometimes we can get him to smile. We give quick hugs and kisses around the table and then I'm out the door by eight a.m.

My first stop most days is Universal Studios Hollywood for a couple of hours behind the microphone of my nationally syndicated radio show, *ON With Mario Lopez*. I work with two smart young producers on the show. Think Beavis and Butt-head, but cleaner. I'm the elder statesman of the group. They keep me young and hip with their snarky and irreverent zingers.

The show is currently number one in LA and in all the major markets for its time slot. I'm proud that we're doing so well and it's probably the one job where I am most free to be me. The great thing about radio is there's such an intimacy when it's just you and the microphone. I get to have a real conversation with America and talk about who I am—Mario, the person—and give my point of view on things. I talk about real stories that are going on between me and my wife, me and my kids, me and the rest of my family, and what's going on with my other jobs. We also discuss celebrities, pop culture, and current events. We cover it all. The best part is that I get to give my personal viewpoint, unfiltered.

I have tons of guests on the show too—a plethora of colorful characters from the world of sports, entertainment, and music. I've had Julia Roberts, Arnold Schwarzenegger, Jenny McCarthy, Will Ferrell, Kim Kardashian, and Britney Spears in the studio. I've had Snooki from *Jersey Shore* and even Mike Tyson on the air with me. Mike Tyson is great because he has that voice that anyone listening instantly recognizes. Brave comedians like to imitate his voice, and I don't blame them, because it's so unique with that lisp and that Brooklyn accent. "Hey, Mario. How you doin'? Are you still gettin' in the ring and beatin' up people, knockin' 'em out?" If you're thinking of mocking his voice, don't forget that he hasn't forgotten how to fight.

When celebrities like Julia Roberts or Arnold Schwarzenegger come on, I try to create that unfiltered free flow that reminds me of all the family gatherings in my upbringing. It's early in the morning but we're able to get the party going with topics and anecdotes as opposed to going down a list of bulleted talking points.

Julia has the best, most infectious laugh around and she can be chatty or serious. She's smart, funny, and obviously talented and beautiful. We might talk about how she got her first break in the biz or what she does to keep balance between her work and her family life. You can't see it on the radio, but when I joke around and tease, Julia gets this playful look in her eye likes she's up to no good. Arnold Schwarzenegger also has the ability to be really funny and also serious. His journey as an entrepreneur is an endless source of fascination to me and I also like that he can make fun of his accent—even making fun of himself by repeating jokes from *Saturday Night Live*, with phrases like "Pump you up!" and "Don't be a girly man!"

Once my radio gig had taken off, the powers that be wanted me to expand and asked for a female voice to enter the fold. I tried out many different female voices, all of them wonderful and all of them veterans of the radio world yet none had the right sass to keep the banter going with me. Well, when it comes to sass, I mean, who better than my wife, right?

Coincidentally, I used to bring my wife in now and then to help out, primarily because I'd always be referring to her on the show: "So, last night my wife was giving me a hard time about not stealing the covers. Tell me if I'm wrong . . ." The fans spoke and I listened. The female audience really responded when Courtney chimed in. Plus, Courtney aka Mazza is not just my wife. She's also incredibly funny, clever, and only too happy to give me a hard time. Not to mention, she has a very soothing radio voice.

There was no question. Mazza was the one. Although I wasn't sure what would happen when I pitched the idea: "What if my wife came in here for a couple of days a week and we recorded some segments together?" The Clear Channel folks loved the idea and my producers love her. So now she is my female cohost. I admit, as much as I love my wife and as much fun as we have doing the show together, I wrestled with the idea for a while. I was initially reluctant because I've heard horror stories of couples trying to work together. Dick Clark always used to say, "You want the quickest way to get a divorce? Work with your wife." But we're not any couple; we're us. We'll be just fine.

And that's the radio show. Luckily, Universal Studios is like ground zero for me. As long as outside meetings or other assignments don't call me away from the lot, most of my job destinations are either walking distance or just a golf cart ride away. So, much of the time, immediately after the radio show I head straight to where we shoot *Extra* and go into hair and makeup. Then I'm off to go "track," which means I have to record voice-over pieces that will air along with the interviews on the show.

Doing voice-over is a skill I've mastered through years of trial and error. I am required to be enthusiastic, know which words to stress, and make sure I read at the correct speed. Sections of the script have times on them. For example, above the line "Jennifer Lawrence was in Las Vegas last week promoting her new film *American Hustle*" would be written the time of 2:30. That means I have to read it in exactly 2.5 seconds. Not 1.9 or 2.15—it has to be 2.5 seconds on the nose. Betty, our soft-spoken but perfectionist sound engineer, will scream, "No—I need it a half second slower!" or "Speed it up one second, Mario." I've gotten used to making those precise corrections and can normally hit my mark within one or two tries.

The big task after voice-overs is starting to do the actual show by shooting the various wraps. "Wrap" is short for "wraparound." Think of them as nice rubber bands that keep the story compact and easily understood. The wraps are the introductions to the interviews that we air on the show and are often staged at different locations at Universal. Either I run on foot to where I'm needed for the wrap or I hop in a golf cart and get there in time to be mic'd up and ready for camera.

On an average day, I'll do three to four interviews with different celebrities. Often, the celebrities will request me specifically. So I get the brunt of the interviews, usually about 95 percent. That means I have to do the interviews *and* I have to do the wraps that go with them. Meanwhile, I am running back and forth to finish updating and completing other pieces for my radio show. So I'll go from three to four, sometimes five interviews with *Extra* during the day, to another two or three interviews for my radio show. I've literally had eight to nine interviews in one day by the time it's all said and done.

My go time that I love is shooting with a live audience at Universal. Most of the people who come to watch us tape and stand in the background are tourists. They're always friendly and provide great energy to all of us working on set. Plus, they get to see some of their favorite stars close up, and they get to see themselves on TV.

One of the things I love most about *Extra* is the family atmosphere we enjoy behind the scenes. There are hundreds of people who work at *Extra* and make it run like clockwork. We tease one another mercilessly and I can take it as well as give it out—thanks to the cast of characters I'm lucky enough to work with each day. The teasing normally involves someone's hairstyle or the way they're dressed. Tuddy gets the brunt of it because he dresses like a gangster from *Goodfellas* and is a straight male makeup artist. We are not above pranking either—prank phone calls on one another, you name it. All in jest.

After my on-set work is done, I get a short break. I try to carve out some time to get a little workout in every day. That's when I'll drive off to the boxing gym. I'll wash off the makeup—there's no way I'm going to a boxing gym in that. Then I'll spar. Why not mix up my workout and a break from the demands of the day to de-stress? It makes me feel better and boosts my energy for what's left on the work agenda.

After returning to Universal, I'll go do whatever interview I have lined up for my NUVO show, *Mario Lopez One on One*, which is sort of my version of *Oprah's Next Chapter*. The show specifically focuses on the Latino world and has given me the chance to interview some great guests—everyone from George Lopez to Eva Longoria and Adrian Gonzalez to Carlos Santana. Like the radio show, the NUVO show allows me to go beyond the script and be myself in conversation about both entertaining and serious questions.

Depending on the day of the week or whether or not I'm in the awards season whirlwind, work may include proceeding to the evening's destination for any guest hosting or judging on my docket. Sometimes these assignments come up last minute and I have to be ready to roll. But never fear, all of that is conveyed dutifully by my tireless, polished assistant, Lisa Blas, who has to keep all things Mario in her brain at all times. She is amazing and keeps me fo-cused and on time, providing the address and location and phone numbers of everyone involved, all the point people, and what the traffic is like getting there. Lisa also coordinates with the rest of Team Lopez who aren't at Universal, as meetings and phone calls arise that I need to take.

When I don't have work scheduled in the evenings, before calling it a day, I try to use the time to catch up on other projects that allow me to push myself further as a host and an entrepreneur. I'm humbled to say that the flow and balance of my career is exactly where I like it to be. Careers rise and fall based on how well you manage them. That's why I'm glad I have Mark Schulman; he's been my manager for over ten years. A lot of people don't really need a manager, but he's done a nice job in helping me facilitate logistics with all the projects I've got going on. So I run all of my business decisions by him. I probably talk to him more than anyone else, three or four times a day.

One of the new projects I'm excited about is a cartoon, *The Chica Show*, for kids to watch, including my own Gia and Nico. I also just got a deal with Telepictures. Other TV projects are in the works with my production company, Viamar. "Via" is the last part of my mom's name, and "Mar" is the first part of mine. Elvia, Mario—so, Viamar, which also means "by the sea." It does seem fitting that Mom gets a shout-out in the company name. After all, she had the plan for me from the start.

When I am asked about balancing work with family, the easy answer is: I just do it. I work at balance as a priority. Though every minute of the day is accounted for, I never forget that my roles as husband and dad come before all the others. That's why I make a point to have breakfast with Mazza and the kids before leaving in the morning and, most of the time, finish up and make my way home around seven p.m., usually in time to have dinner with my family, and, best of all, be there to tuck the kids in with Mazza.

How I got so lucky, I don't know but I've never been happier, personally or professionally, than I am at this very moment. I love my family, I'm blessed with a great woman in my life; she's an amazing wife and just a fantastic mom. My parents are still with me. One set of grandparents is still with me. What a joy it is to have them watching Gia and Dominic come into the world and thrive.

It's true: I love what I do for a living. But I'm happiest when I'm with the people I care most about, my family and my friends, drinking, being festive, having lots of food, and being in the comfort of our home. Simple. Yes, I have so much to be thankful for, including the company that you've given me as fans over the years as we grew up together and as I've recalled the journey to this place in time—which brings me full circle and leads me to the parting thoughts that follow.

# JUST BETWEEN US

Over the course of writing this book, I had a few occasions to go for a hike or run at Griffith Park again. Each time I passed the "You Are Here" sign, I realized that I was no longer getting ready to turn forty but that I would soon turn forty-one, right around the time that Dominic turns one. As much as thinking about the past has helped me make sense of how I got here, I've also been thinking a lot about the future.

You can never tell what the future holds and, quite frankly, no matter what I plan, the future will unfold as it will. I think the future is more like a river that meanders and is sometimes fast, sometimes deep, sometimes shallow, and sometimes empties into a huge lake before carrying on. I think turning forty was sort of like my big lake. I'll rest here a minute, take in the sights, and then venture off into the next chapter of my life. This was never where I thought I'd be long ago—that's for sure—so I'll just let the next leg of the journey be an adventure and surprise me.

Still, at this age, living in our complicated times, we start to ask ourselves deeper questions about life: What was I put on the planet for? What is my purpose?

Everybody goes through a point in their life where they try to find out not only the meaning of life but their meaning within life. I'm at that stage now. I got to that point and I turned more to spirituality for answers than to science fiction. Right or wrong, spirituality gives me comfort; it gives me strength, and I've tried to build on that spiritual muscle as I've gotten older. At the end of the day, I know I'm here for a finite amount of time and I try to be the best person I can by doing the right things and hoping the best can happen for me and my family. I'd rather live my life as if there is a God, and if I die and find out there isn't, fine.

I've had occasion to contemplate death over the years. I've lost friends and family members much too young and I want to believe that their loss has made me value life more. Am I afraid of dying and do I know what death is? Yes and no.

I try to focus my thoughts and energy on living and I always have given life my undivided attention.

Why worry? After all, I plan to live until I'm one hundred and twenty years old, so I guess I can think about death when I'm eighty or ninety. I want to take care of myself and I want to live as long as I can. I have every intention of embracing medicine and all the wonderful things that it has to offer if it will keep me alive and healthy.

Age is truly just a number. My advice to myself and to you too: avoid thinking you have to act your age. Be mature and responsible, but feel free to act sixty at twenty years old and act twelve at forty, and so on.

If I've learned anything from taking the time to look back and retrace my footsteps back to the past and to return here to the present and the "You Are Here" sign, I realize that having a sense of purpose is vital. What drives me every day is bigger than me and mine. It's about empowering others in general and about shaking up the Latino business community to do more for each other. In show business, the African-American community has shown how this can be done: by being proactive and supporting one another's work and creating jobs for one another. In the past, the Latino community in Hollywood has not been as cohesive nor sought the kind of unity needed to gain better representation in the various entertainment arenas.

Latinos, I sometimes find, have a little success and then separate themselves from their other Latino friends in the business. I don't know where that separation comes from—whether it's the machismo thing, pride, or hunger—but it can come across as an attitude of "You know what? I got mine; good luck getting yours." We could do well to follow the lead of other groups that support one another, like the Jewish community or the African-American community; these groups have been able to rise together while looking out for one another. We need to come together and help employ our own as well.

I think this is changing little by little, but considering our massive population, our professional network should be a lot further along. We need a Latin version of LinkedIn. I want to help bring us closer and I'm very proud to say that I've gotten countless friends and cousins jobs in the business. And they've made me proud. They are making something big out of entry-level jobs like production assistants or they're doing well moving up the food chain and helping other Latino Americans.

Another passion I have is encouraging all of us in all communities to read more. A book can be an e-ticket. There's magic, there's imagination, and you can totally change the way you see the world by reading one wonderful author. There was a song by the band Tears for Fears that spoke about all you can read in books ... "in the crannies and the nooks, there are books to read." Education is power. The more you read, the more you know; the more you are able to eloquently express yourself, the better you'll do in this world.

Reading has opened many doors for me in my life. And I can now say, with this book, that writing has been a real catharsis that has let me reclaim certain lessons that I'd forgotten—reflections and insights that I hope in some way have touched you, maybe even inspired you. I have a few more insights that I'd like to share with you here at the end. At the top of the list is not to take relationships or family for granted. As you've seen, I'm big on telling people in words that you love them, without saving it for the right time, because if you don't, you may never have the chance. If things need to be done or should be done, do them now, in this very moment, because this very moment is for sure. Life keeps moving forward and things always come up. Plans change. Stay focused and as early as you can try to find whatever it is that you're passionate about and commit to it; believe in yourself no matter how many people say no, and stick to it. Because it's the only way you're going to be able to have any sort of chance of success, and ultimately be happy.

I've learned that there are a lot of people in your life who are important at different times for different reasons, but there are very few who really matter in the big picture, very few who will be with you throughout the good and the bad. I've found it's important to slow down and take stock of the people I've accumulated along the way, and ask myself two important questions: 1) Do they have my best interests at heart? 2) Is my friendship offering them anything valuable?

I've learned that I should try to do a better job of showing those people who have gone out of their way for me that I know the difference between someone who is "phoning it in" and someone who wants to live up to the trust I've been given.

As far as work ethic goes, I'm all for working hard to achieve, and even surpass, your goals. But I've come to see that you should work to live and not just live to work. It can be important and fulfilling, but it's not the be-all and end-all of your life. It's not what matters. No one will be lying on their deathbed wishing they'd worked longer and harder.

Here's a big one: it's not about quantity; it's about quality. Money and material possessions will never make me as happy as seeing something as simple as Gia's smile, hugging my son Dominic, hearing Mazza laugh, or seeing my friends stuff their faces in my house.

Try not to force love or marriage, or succumb to pressures because your friends are doing it and you think it's time to have a family. Be patient. The only thing you should focus on and keep working on is yourself and your personal growth. The family, the love—all that will come when you are the best *you* you can be. You work on yourself, you do the right thing, I think God will provide the rest for you and fill in the blanks.

At night, no matter how tired I am, no matter how hungover I am, no matter what, I always try to drop to my knees and give thanks. Each night when I pray, the first thing I do is ask forgiveness for any transgressions. I ask to not make the same mistakes over. I pray for the strength to overcome struggles.

I strive to have the wisdom to make the right choices so that the right things can happen for my family and me. I give thanks and appreciation for all the wonderful blessings: my health, my family, everything I have. I tell God how grateful and appreciative I am. I ask Him to take care of my wife and my kids and to help me be the parent, the father, and the provider I aim to be. To always come from a place of love, especially with the people I love. I ask Him to take care of my mom and dad, my sister and her family. I try to apply the Four Agreements: 1) to be impeccable with my word, 2) to not take things personally, 3) to not assume anything, and

4) to always do my best. I end my prayers with a Hail Mary and an Our Father, and I go to bed. When I wake up, I just say a quick prayer to help me through my day and I'm on my way.

As you can see, it's been a wild ride these last forty years. Thank you for sitting down and giving me the kindness of your ear as I've roamed the halls of the past. You've let me savor some wonderful memories and shed a tear or two for the ones who aren't here to continue on with us. Thank you for being a guest on this show called my life. Let's keep these stories just between us.

XO, Mario.

# ACKNOWLEDGMENTS

Saying *thank you* is often more important than saying please. The level of gratitude I have for everyone involved in helping me on my path from childhood to forty years old is enormous. Notwithstanding, is there anything worse than an Oscar speech that goes on far too long, mentioning people none of us know? With you in mind, I will keep this brief. Rest assured that you are in my mind, and that I thank you wholeheartedly, even if you're not singled out below. Thank you all!

Ray Garcia, Publisher ~ I love working with you! This is our fourth book together and each one has been a great pleasure! I look forward to continuing many more years of work and friendship.

Jennifer Schuster, Senior Editor ~ My patient confidante who, through her infinite wisdom, kept *Just Between Us* on course.

Steve Santagati, writer ~ For your writing, interview skills, friendship, insight, and patience throughout this process—they have proven to be a priceless commodity.

Mark Schulman, my longtime manager ~ For organizing the sum of parts so that they, once again, make a whole.

Mim Eichler Rivas ~ The "book doctor" who made sure our "body of work" functioned in a healthy way!

And thank you to everyone behind the scenes at the publishing level for all of your expertise and help!

To Lisa Gregorisch-Dempsey aka "Carmela," Extra-Senior Executive Producer ~ Without your guidance, belief, patience, wisdom, and support, I wouldn't be where I am today. Thank you for keeping me in the game and winning. You'll always be my Belichick, and I'll be your Brady.

And of course, Fatana Nawabi, our managing editor at *Extra* ~ Thank you for the great title suggestion for my book!

Thank you to EVERYONE on the *Extra* team! I appreciate each and every one of you for all that you put into making my job a blast and our show the best!

Thank you to Clear Channel and my team at *On With Mario*.

To Lisa Blas, the best assistant in the world ~ Without her none of the "I's" would have dots nor would the "T's" be crossed.

To all of my cousins, extended family, and friends ~ You guys rock! I love having all of you in my life, and your loyalty and support are unparalleled. *Mi casa* will always be *su casa*. Thank you all from the bottom of my heart.

To my sister, Marissa ~ I couldn't have asked for a better or more loving sister. Thank you for being the best friend a brother could have.

To my father ~ You've helped me go from a boy to a man, and I appreciate everything you sacrificed to get me here! Thank you, Dad!

To my mother ~ You are my rock! I love you more than I am able to express in words. You've done so much for me, I wouldn't know where to begin. All I will say is this: If everyone had a mother like you, the world would be a much better place. Love you.

To my incredibly beautiful and talented wife, Courtney ~ You and our amazing children are my world. Your love, affection, and support are what give meaning to my life. Without you all of my success wouldn't be nearly as sweet. Though I don't look forward to growing old, I look forward to being by your side the entire way.